Published in this series:

Guy Cook: *Applied Linguistics*
Rod Ellis: *Second Language Acquisition*
Claire Kramsch: *Language and Culture*
Tim McNamara: *Language Testing*
Peter Roach: *Phonetics*
Herbert Schendl: *Historical Linguistics*
Tom Scovel: *Psycholinguistics*
Bernard Spolsky: *Sociolinguistics*
Michael Swan: *Grammar*
Peter Verdonk: *Stylistics*
H. G. Widdowson: *Linguistics*
George Yule: *Pragmatics*

Oxford Introductions to Language Study

Series Editor H.G.Widdowson

Discourse Analysis

H. G. Widdowson

OXFORD
UNIVERSITY PRESS

OXFORD
UNIVERSITY PRESS

Great Clarendon Street, Oxford OX2 6DP

Oxford University Press is a department of the University of Oxford.
It furthers the University's objective of excellence in research, scholarship,
and education by publishing worldwide in

Oxford New York

Auckland Cape Town Dar es Salaam Hong Kong Karachi
Kuala Lumpur Madrid Melbourne Mexico City Nairobi
New Delhi Shanghai Taipei Toronto

With offices in

Argentina Austria Brazil Chile Czech Republic France Greece
Guatemala Hungary Italy Japan Poland Portugal Singapore
South Korea Switzerland Thailand Turkey Ukraine Vietnam

OXFORD and OXFORD ENGLISH are registered trade marks of
Oxford University Press in the UK and in certain other countries

ISBN-13: 978 0 19 438921 1

Printed in China

For Cristina Whitecross

Contents

Preface

Purpose

What justification might there be for a series of introductions to language study? After all, linguistics is already well served with introductory texts: expositions and explanations which are comprehensive, authoritative, and excellent in their way. Generally speaking, however, their way is the essentially academic one of providing a detailed initiation into the discipline of linguistics, and they tend to be lengthy and technical: appropriately so, given their purpose. But they can be quite daunting to the novice. There is also a need for a more general and gradual introduction to language: transitional texts which will ease people into an understanding of complex ideas. This series of introductions is designed to serve this need.

Their purpose, therefore, is not to supplant but to support the more academically oriented introductions to linguistics: to prepare the conceptual ground. They are based on the belief that it is an advantage to have a broad map of the terrain sketched out before one considers its more specific features on a smaller scale, a general context in reference to which the detail makes sense. It is sometimes the case that students are introduced to detail without it being made clear what it is a detail of. Clearly, a general understanding of ideas is not sufficient: there needs to be closer scrutiny. But equally, close scrutiny can be myopic and meaningless unless it is related to the larger view. Indeed it can be said that the precondition of more particular enquiry is an awareness of what, in general, the particulars are about. This series is designed to provide this large-scale view of different areas of language study.

As such it can serve as preliminary to (and precondition for) the more specific and specialized enquiry which students of linguistics are required to undertake.

But the series is not only intended to be helpful to such students. There are many people who take an interest in language without being academically engaged in linguistics per se. Such people may recognize the importance of understanding language for their own lines of enquiry, or for their own practical purposes, or quite simply for making them aware of something which figures so centrally in their everyday lives. If linguistics has revealing and relevant things to say about language, this should presumably not be a privileged revelation, but one accessible to people other than linguists. These books have been so designed as to accommodate these broader interests too: they are meant to be introductions to language more generally as well as to linguistics as a discipline.

Design

The books in the series are all cut to the same basic pattern. There are four parts: Survey, Readings, References, and Glossary.

Survey

This is a summary overview of the main features of the area of language study concerned: its scope and principles of enquiry, its basic concerns and key concepts. These are expressed and explained in ways which are intended to make them as accessible as possible to people who have no prior knowledge or expertise in the subject. The Survey is written to be readable and is uncluttered by the customary scholarly references. In this sense, it is simple. But it is not simplistic. Lack of specialist expertise does not imply an inability to understand or evaluate ideas. Ignorance means lack of knowledge, not lack of intelligence. The Survey, therefore, is meant to be challenging. It draws a map of the subject area in such a way as to stimulate thought and to invite a critical participation in the exploration of ideas. This kind of conceptual cartography has its dangers of course: the selection of what is significant, and the manner of its representation, will not be to the liking of everybody, particularly not, perhaps, to some of those inside the discipline. But these surveys are written in the belief that there must be an alternative to a technical account on the one hand and an idiot's guide on the other if linguistics is to be made relevant to people in the wider world.

Readings

Some people will be content to read, and perhaps reread, the summary Survey. Others will want to pursue the subject and so will use the Survey as the preliminary for more detailed study. The Readings provide the necessary transition. For here the reader is presented with texts extracted from the specialist literature. The purpose of these Readings is quite different from the Survey. It is to get readers to focus on the specifics of what is said, and how it is said, in these source texts. Questions are provided to further this purpose: they are designed to direct attention to points in each text, how they compare across texts, and how they deal with the issues discussed in the Survey. The idea is to give readers an initial familiarity with the more specialist idiom of the linguistics literature, where the issues might not be so readily accessible, and to encourage them into close critical reading.

References

One way of moving into more detailed study is through the Readings. Another is through the annotated References in the third section of each book. Here there is a selection of works (books and articles) for further reading. Accompanying comments indicate how these deal in more detail with the issues discussed in the different chapters of the Survey.

Glossary

Certain terms in the Survey appear in bold. These are terms used in a special or technical sense in the discipline. Their meanings are made clear in the discussion, but they are also explained in the Glossary at the end of each book. The Glossary is cross-referenced to the Survey, and therefore serves at the same time as an index. This enables readers to locate the term and what it signifies in the more general discussion, thereby, in effect, using the Survey as a summary work of reference.

Use

The series has been designed so as to be flexible in use. Each title is separate and self-contained, with only the basic format in common. The four sections of the format, as described here, can be drawn upon and combined in different ways, as required by the needs, or interests, of different readers. Some may be content with the Survey and the Glossary and may not want to follow up the suggested References. Some may not wish to venture into the Readings. Again, the Survey might be considered as appropriate preliminary reading for a course in applied linguistics or teacher education, and the Readings more appropriate for seminar discussion during the course. In short, the notion of an introduction will mean different things to different people, but in all cases the concern is to provide access to specialist knowledge and stimulate an awareness of its significance. This series as a whole has been designed to provide this access and promote this awareness in respect to different areas of language study.

H. G. WIDDOWSON

Author's Preface

A note on what is covered in this book.

As is appropriate for a title in this particular series, this book is about discourse as an area of language study. As such it is concerned with how the encoded resources available in a language are put to communicative use. The study of discourse in this sense is a general enquiry into how people make meaning, and make *out* meaning, in texts.

But the term 'discourse' can be understood in rather a different way. The meanings that people make are not only constrained by the language they know but also by the social group or community they belong to. Meanings are socio-cultural constructs of reality: they represent particular beliefs and values that define ways of thinking about the world. The study of discourse in this case would focus not so much on how meanings are linguistically realized in texts, as on how they are socially constructed so that expressing them is effectively a kind of social practice.

The two ways of thinking of discourse are not mutually exclusive, of course. It is more a matter of emphasis. This book takes more of a linguistic than a sociological perspective and focuses on discourse as language use, although the notion of discourse as social practice comes into the discussion in Section 1 and references to work that adopts this perspective is provided in Section 3.

A note of thanks.

Parts of the content of this book made their first appearance in lectures I have given over the years to students in the Universities of Edinburgh, London, Essex and Vienna. These students, of course, need no introduction to discourse analysis, but should they ever happen to browse in this book, they might find some of it familiar. Though they are not responsible for the book's deficiencies, they can take a good deal of credit for whatever merits it has: for in teaching a subject, it is the reactions of students that tell you how far you have succeeded in making it accessible and engaging. So my thanks to them in general.

And my special thanks to two of them in particular, Guy Cook and Barbara Seidlhofer, who, in a nice reversal of roles, have long since guided me in my thinking. Guy Cook, himself distinguished as a writer on discourse, was good enough to read through an earlier draft of this book, and to point out shortcomings that I tried to remedy. The influence of Barbara Seidlhofer is all pervasive in this book, as it is in all other things I do in my personal and professional life.

Finally, my thanks to somebody who has never been my student, but who has worked with me as a close and supportive colleague and friend for many years: Cristina Whitecross. This book is dedicated to her.

HGW
Vienna, September 2006

Survey

1
Language in use

A sample of language

Given a sample of language, there are all kinds of things we can say about it. Take, for example, a familiar public notice:

KEEP OFF THE GRASS

This, to begin with, is something in English, as distinct from French or Arabic or Chinese or any other language. It consists of four words, all in capital letters, and all, we might more expertly add, monosyllabic. If we have been fortunate enough to have had some instruction in linguistics, we might then go on point out that the words combine to form a grammatical unit called a **sentence**, and a sentence furthermore of an imperative as distinct from a declarative or interrogative kind consisting of two main **constituents.** The first is a verb phrase consisting of the two words *keep off*, the second a noun phrase which itself consists of two constituents, a definite article *the* and a noun *grass*. Noting these grammatical features, we might think up a number of other sentences that seem to be structured in the same way: *Put out the light*, for example, or *Turn off the tap*, only to realize perhaps that appearances are deceptive and that these are actually not quite the same, but interestingly different. For these two structures can also take the form of the alternative sequences *Put the light out*, *Turn the tap off*, but *Keep the grass off* will not do. So examining the properties of this sample of ours as a sentence might lead us into a fascinating excursion into the mysteries of grammatical analysis.

But although linguists might delight in examining our sample in this way, this is not the kind of thing people would customarily do. Languages are traditionally recorded for us in analytic terms:

grammars display the range of possible structural combinations in sentences, and dictionaries provide us with the meanings of words separated out and listed in alphabetic order. These can be said to represent the encoded resources of form and meaning that speakers of a particular language know and draw upon intuitively when they use it. But they do not correspond with how speakers actually experience it as use. When they come across a public notice, they do not see it as a sample of language and analyse it into its formal constituents. They take note of it only to the extent that they recognize its purpose, as something not to analyse but to act upon. In other words they treat it as a **text**.

What is a text?

A text can be defined as an actual use of language, as distinct from a sentence which is an abstract unit of linguistic analysis. We identify a piece of language as a text as soon as we recognize that it has been produced for a communicative purpose. But we can identify a text as a purposeful use of language without necessarily being able to interpret just what is meant by it. It is a fairly common experience to come across texts in an unknown language which we nevertheless recognize as public notices, food labels, menus, or operating instructions, and to be frustrated by the inability to understand them. Clearly we would generally need to know the language a text is in to be able to interpret it. But this is not the only condition on interpretation. We may know what the language means but still not understand what is meant by its use in a particular text.

Consider again the public notice 'KEEP OFF THE GRASS'. We may know well enough what the word *grass* **denotes** (and should we be in any doubt we can consult a dictionary to find out). But what the word denotes is not the same as knowing what it is meant to **refer** to when it occurs here in the phrase *the grass*. The definite article *the* signals that what is being referred to is a matter of shared knowledge. The grass. But which grass? Obviously, one might say, the grass in the vicinity of the notice. So what we do is to establish reference by relating the text to the **context** in which it is located. But then the question arises as to how far this vicinity is meant to extend. Does *the grass* refer just to the particular patch where the notice is placed, or to other patches nearby as well, or to the whole park? The range of reference is not specified in the language itself. We make assumptions about what it is on the basis of what we know about public notices of this kind and how they are conventionally meant to be understood. In other words we relate the text not only to the actual situational context in which we find it, but to the abstract cultural context of what we know to be conventional.

And by relating text to context we infer not only what the notice refers to, but also what its purpose is. We recognize that it is intended as a prohibition, although whether we choose to pay any attention to it is another matter—and one we shall be taking up later.

The same point can be made about other notices we come across in daily life. Thus we recognize that the texts 'HANDLE WITH CARE' or 'THIS SIDE UP' refer to a container on which they are written and function as requests, that 'WET PAINT' refers to some surface in the immediate vicinity that has been newly painted, and functions as a warning. Similarly, when we see the label 'KEEP AWAY FROM CHILDREN' on a medicine bottle, we take this as a specific warning in reference to the particular contents of the bottle, rather than, say, as a piece of general advice to keep clear of young people at all times. When we come across notices and labels, then, we make sense of them by relating the language to the immediate perceptual context where they are located, and to the conceptual context of our knowledge of how such texts are designed to function. We cannot make sense out of them simply by focusing on the language itself. In the case of simple texts like notices and labels, establishing the language-context connections is usually a fairly straightforward matter. With other texts, even apparently simple ones, making such connections is not so easy, as anybody who has had the experience of assembling furniture from a set of instructions is likely to testify.

Text and discourse

The simple texts we have been considering so far all serve an obvious utilitarian purpose: notices, labels, instructions are designed to be directly acted upon and to get things done. But of course not all texts are so simple in form or so straightforward in function. Although, as we have seen, not all texts extend beyond the sentence, a great many of them do: travel guides, information leaflets, newspaper articles, interviews, speeches, reports, poems, and so on. Some of these have an obvious utility function but others are meant to serve a range of different social purposes: to give information, express a point of view, shape opinion, provide entertainment, and so on. These functions, furthermore, are frequently combined in complex ways: a travel guide, for example, may provide information, but is also designed to promote the attractions it describes; and what is presented as a factual account in a newspaper article will usually reflect, and promote, a particular point of view.

Whether simple or complex, all texts are uses of language which are produced with the intention to refer to something for some purpose. We identify a stretch of language as a text when we recognize this intention, and there are times when the intention is made explicit as when a text is labelled as a *notice*, or *instructions*, or *report* or *proclamation*. But recognizing a text is not the same as realizing its meaning. You may not know what is being referred to in a particular text, or in part of a text; or you may know full well what is being referred to, but fail to see what communicative purpose lies behind the reference. In the case of simple texts, like public notices, it will be a straightforward matter to match up intention with interpretation, but in the case of more complex ones, like newspaper articles, such matching can, as we shall see later, prove to be highly problematic.

People produce texts to get a message across, to express ideas and beliefs, to explain something, to get other people to do certain things or to think in a certain way, and so on. We can refer to this complex of communicative purposes as the **discourse** that underlies the text and motivates its production in the first place. But at the receiving end readers or listeners then have to make meaning out of the text to make it a communicative reality. In other words, they have to interpret the text as a discourse that makes sense to them. Texts, in this view, do not contain meaning, but are used to mediate it across discourses. Sometimes, of course, as with the notices we have been considering, the mediation is relatively straightforward: what the text means to the reader will generally match up with what the producer of the text meant by it. Obviously we must generally assume that texts will serve to mediate some convergence between discourses, or otherwise no communication would take place at all, but, as we shall see, the degree of convergence varies a good deal. As we all know from our own experience, no matter how explicitly we think we have **textualized** what we want to say, there is always the possibility that it will be interpreted otherwise.

So the term **discourse** is taken here to refer both to what a text producer meant by a text and what a text means to the receiver. Of course what somebody means by producing a particular text may well relate to broader issues of what social and ideological values they subscribe to, and another way of thinking of discourse is indeed to focus on such broader issues and look at how texts can be used to express, and impose, certain ways of thinking about the world. This is something we shall return to later in the book (in Chapter 7).

Spoken and written text

For the moment, the point to be made is that texts are the perceptible traces of the process, not itself open to direct perception, of mediating a message. In conversation, these traces are typically fragmented and ephemeral, and disappear as soon as they are produced to serve their immediate discourse purpose. They can, of course, be recorded, but do not need to be, and usually are not. Thus, participants in spoken interaction produce and process text as they go along and there is no need for it to be retained as a record for it to mediate their discourse, and this mediation is regulated on-line to negotiate whatever convergence between intention and interpretation is required for the purpose. Written text, on the other hand, is not jointly constructed and construed on-line in this way. It is typically designed and recorded unilaterally in the act of production by one of the participants, the writer, as a completed expression of the intended message. The text is then taken up and interpreted as a separate process. The mediation, therefore, is displaced and delayed and this obviously will often make a convergence between intention and interpretation more difficult to achieve.

And there is a further difficulty. When people communicate they do not only produce linguistic texts. In speech, they make use not only of language but of **paralanguage**—tones of voice, varying stress, pauses, and so on, and what they say is accompanied by facial expression, or gesture, as part of the message they intend to get across. In written communication, too, how a text is given a particular shape by choice of typeface, or its arrangement on a page, may suggest significance over and above what it signifies linguistically. And it may be **multimodal** in that the text is accompanied by, and related to, other modes of communication —pictures, diagrams, charts, and so on.

It is the lack of direct correspondence between text and discourse that makes communication so indeterminate, and so intriguing. Life would in some ways be much easier if we could pin things down more precisely, if all we needed to do to communicate was to assemble a combination of linguistic forms of fixed meaning and transmit them for dismantling at the receiving end. A text would then signal its own meaning, whatever the context or purpose of its production. But when we use language we do not just present the meanings that are encoded in it, we exploit them as a potential resource for making meaning of our own. The encoded meanings are **semantic meanings** and are what are described in dictionaries and grammar books. To know a language is to know what they are. But in using a language we not only put this knowledge on display but also act upon it as appropriate to our communicative intentions: in other words we always make this semantic meaning serve a **pragmatic** purpose.

Illustration from a crowded train

To illustrate: let us suppose that you overhear the following **utterance** in a conversation between two people in a crowded train.

He has put it in a safe place and it will not be found.

As linguistic data, we might note that as far as grammar is concerned this is a complete and well formed sentence of English. The present perfect in the first half (*has put*) and the passive in the second (*will ... be found*) are produced in conformity with grammatical rule, there is agreement, as required, between the singular pronoun *he* and the following verb, the past tense forms are morphologically well formed (*put* not *putted*, *found* not *finded*), word order is as it should be, and so on. As far as **lexis** is concerned, we can attest that the words that occur in the sentence are quite normal English ones (*put, safe, place, find*). But we do not only recognize that this is a regular and well formed example of English. Since we know what semantic meaning is signified by the grammatical and lexical forms we have recognized, we are able to decode what has been encoded and assign it a meaning, as a sentence. However, we are still in the dark about what this person is actually talking about. Who is 'he' and what is 'it'? These pronouns have an established denotation: *he* encodes the **semantic features** of singular and masculine, and *it* the semantic features of singular and inanimate. But although a knowledge of these denotations narrows down the possibilities, it does not tell you who or what is being referred to. What is meant by the language will continue to be pragmatically elusive.

This utterance is, of course, only a fragment of conversation, one piece of the text, that the two people in the train are producing in the process of enacting their discourse. They know what they are talking about because they have established the context of shared knowledge and assumption that the actual language they produce keys into. If we are not a party to this context and only have the linguistic trace of their discourse to go by, we cannot interpret what they mean by what they say. When they leave the train, they take their meaning with them, and we will not be able to recover it, no matter how closely we analyse the actual language.

Conclusion

To summarize. When people communicate with each other, they draw on the semantic resources encoded in their language to key into a context they assume to be shared so as to enact a discourse, that is, to get their intended message across to some second person party. The linguistic trace of this process is the text. In the case of conversation, the text is jointly produced as the discourse proceeds by overt interaction, and it typically disappears once it has served its purpose. In the case of writing the text is unilaterally produced and remains as a permanent record. But it is still only a discourse trace, and what is meant by it has to be inferred by interpretation, and this inevitably raises the question of how far this interpretation corresponds with the intentions that informed the discourse which gave rise to the text in the first place.

In the normal circumstances of use, of course, we only pay attention to text in order to realize its discourse function and so we tend to think of the two as the same thing, as indeed do some linguists, and talk about the meaning of a text as shorthand for what it means to us or what it might mean to the writer or speaker. But although we normally experience text as part of the discourse process, it is perfectly possible to focus on the text alone. This is after all what proofreaders generally do when they scrutinize a piece of writing to identify typographical errors, or wordings that do not conform to established code conventions. More interestingly, texts can also be subjected to close analytic study to find out patterns of actual usage which those producing them may be quite unaware of, an area of linguistic description we shall be returning to in a later chapter. But before we get on to this, it will be necessary to say a little more about how the concepts introduced in this chapter—semantic and pragmatic meaning, sentence, utterance, text, context, and discourse— figure in a general model of communication.

2

Communication

Grammar and communication

As was pointed out at the beginning of the first chapter, linguists have traditionally focused their attention primarily on the internal properties of languages, on how meaning is **formally encoded** in lexis and grammar. The description of such properties can be said to be an account of what people know of their language, an account of their **linguistic competence**. It was this competence that enabled us to describe the grammatical features of the utterance in the train in the preceding chapter. Of course that description made use of terminology which might well be unfamiliar with people competent in English: knowing the grammar of a language is not the same as knowing how to describe it—that is the business of the grammarian. But the point is that anybody competent in English would recognize that the utterance conforms to the **encoding conventions** of the standard language, that it exemplifies a well formed sentence in English, which it would not do if it had taken the form, for example:

They has it in a safe place put and it will not to find.

The original utterance, we can say, exemplifies a possible sentence in English and this second one does not.

So on hearing this remark in the train, one judgement we can make on the basis of our linguistic competence is whether it is grammatically and lexically possible or not, that is to say, in accordance with the encoding conventions of the language. But we can also recognize degrees of possibility. So if the utterance had been:

They has put it in a safe place and it will not be found.

We would recognize that this is a closer approximation to the standard language. Indeed, an utterance like this might be perfectly possible in a non-standard variety of English. We have to note that we make judgements about what is possible in English only by reference to some agreed norm or other. So in the English that I myself spoke as a boy, *you was* and *he were* are grammatically possible, whereas the standard forms *you were* and *he was* are not. Usually, however, for reasons we shall touch on later, it is the standard that serves as the norm of **grammatical well-formedness**.

However, although linguists may take particular notice of such features of a linguistic form, ordinary language users generally focus their attention on what is meant by the use of such forms, and this, as we have seen, involves taking context into account. So another judgement that might be made about an instance of language use is whether and to what extent it is **appropriate** to its context. The issue here is not whether a piece of language is grammatically or lexically well formed as a sentence or not but how far it is pragmatically effective as an act of communication.

Three kinds of pragmatic meaning

Acts of communication can be pragmatically effective in three ways. First, the language can be used to talk about something, to express a **proposition** of some kind. This involves making a connection with context in such a way as to make an appropriate **reference**. Let us suppose, for example, that the following is part of the text of a conversation:

The taxi will be here in a quarter of an hour.

The definite article provides an appropriate contextual connection since it signals that what is being referred to is common knowledge between the people engaged in the conversation (*The taxi we talked about, the taxi you asked me to order ...*). The adverb *here*, and the prepositional phrase *in a quarter of an hour*, locate the utterance in a particular context of place and time that the participants share. Without these contextual co-ordinates, the referential possibilities of this expression would, of course, be endless (*here* could be anywhere, *in a quarter of an hour*, any time). To the extent that the conversationalists recognize the co-ordinates, appropriate reference is achieved.

One kind of pragmatic meaning, then, is reference, but it is not the only kind. The person who utters this expression is not just referring to a future state of affairs, but is doing so in the process of performing a kind of communicative or **illocutionary act**. This, for example, might be a promise (*I have arranged everything. The taxi will be here in a quarter of an hour*), or advice (*You should pack your bags. The taxi will be here in a quarter of an hour*). Whether the utterance is intended as having the **illocutionary force** of promise, or advice, or anything else, will again depend on the context of knowledge and assumption that the speaker assumes to be shared.

To the extent that this expression makes an appropriate connection with context, then, it can he taken as having a certain reference and a certain force. But the speaker is doing something else as well. The speaker is not just acting, but acting *upon* the other person, to bring about a certain state of mind or course of action. In performing an illocutionary act, she is also bringing about a **perlocutionary effect**. In promising, she or he may be intending to reassure the other person (*Don't worry, I have arranged everything ...*), or the advice may be meant to stir him/her into action (*Hurry up!*)

We shall be returning to these kinds of pragmatic meaning in a later chapter, but the point to be made at present is that our recognition of the extent to which a piece of language keys into context appropriately so as to acquire a certain reference, force, and effect requires more than linguistic knowledge. We may be able to assign semantic meaning to a particular expression as a sentence but be quite unable to make pragmatic sense of it as an utterance, as an instance of language use. Knowing what a *sentence* means is one thing, but knowing what is meant by an *utterance* is another. The two are of course related: our knowledge of the encoded possibilities in the language delimits the range of pragmatic interpretation. So it is that in our example, our linguistic knowledge about what the word *taxi* denotes as a **lexical item** in English, and knowing that the definite article *the* signals shared knowledge, provide crucial pointers as to what the speaker is referring to. Our ability to infer what somebody is doing with the language on any particular occasion will to some degree depend on our knowing what is encoded in the language itself, even though it is not determined by it. Our ability to communicate, our **communicative competence**, therefore, incorporates both a knowledge of what is encoded as possible in the language and a knowledge of how these encodings are used appropriately in context.

Four aspects of communicative competence

What is **possible** in the language, in the sense of what can be encoded in it, and what is appropriate in its use are two factors that are included in the well-known account of communicative competence proposed by the American scholar Dell Hymes. He includes two other factors in his account. One of these is **feasibility**. Our competence in a language, he argues, includes our recognition of the extent to which a particular expression can be readily processed. A piece of language might be a grammatically and lexically possible encoding in the language, but difficult to decipher. An example often given of this is of the multiple embedding of one structure in another. Thus the sentence *The dog chased the cat* can be grammatically rewritten, or transformed, into *This is the cat the dog chased*. Another sentence, *The cat killed the rat*, can then be embedded to form *This is the rat the cat the dog chased killed*. This already poses something of a problem, but if we go on to embed another sentence—*The rat ate the corn*—the resulting structure becomes almost impossible to process: *This is the corn the rat the cat the dog chased killed ate*. Though this can be taken as a possible structure in English, since it conforms to encoding conventions, it will also be recognized as relatively unfeasible. This is, of course, an extreme example, and one might object that although linguists might amuse themselves by inventing such structures, they are so perversely complex that it is unlikely that they would ever actually occur. But the point about feasibility can also be illustrated by kinds of structure that are by no means uncommon, namely those we recognize as ambiguous. **Ambiguity** occurs when two distinct structures converge into one single sequence of sentence constituents, as in the well-known example:

To visit aunts can be boring   Aunts who visit can be boring

Visiting aunts can be boring.

The ambiguous sentence is grammatically entirely well formed but lacks feasibility in that it can be decoded in two completely different but equally valid ways. This, it is true, is an invented example but, unlike the embedded structures considered earlier, ambiguities of this kind are well attested in actual texts. Here are two examples:

Two sisters were reunited after eight years at a
checkout counter.

The stolen painting was found by a tree.

Perfectly possible expressions in a language may, then, be relatively lacking in feasibility. Conversely, an expression may be entirely feasible in that it is easy to process, but not be grammatically well formed and so not possible with regard to the encoding conventions of the language. This is commonly the case with the utterances of spoken text which tend to dispense with grammatical features that are surplus to pragmatic requirement, although Mr Jingle, a character in Dickens' *The Pickwick Papers* perhaps takes this tendency to extremes:

'Mr Pickwick—deepest obligations—life preserver—made a
man of me—you shall never repent it, sir.'
'I'm happy to hear you say so,' said Mr Pickwick. 'You look
much better.'
'Thanks to you, sir—great change—Majesty's Fleet—
unwholesome place—very,' said Jingle.

Here, Jingle's fragments of talk are easy to process: they are feasible enough.

The general point to be made, then, is that there is no direct correspondence between feasibility and grammatical well-formedness, any more than there is between grammatical well-formedness and appropriateness to context. The extent to which an expression is possible, processible, and appropriate are three separate things. One of the central questions that discourse analysis needs to consider is how they are related in actual use, and we shall be taking up this issue in later chapters.

But meanwhile we have a fourth factor to consider. Hymes suggests that to be communicatively competent in a language we must be capable not only of recognizing how far an instance of it is possible, feasible, and appropriate but also how far it is actually **performed** or produced, the extent of its frequency of occurrence. The language code provides the basic resources for communication, but we do not, of course, make use of these resources in equal measure. We may, for example, know the words *walk* and *perambulate*, and both will be listed in a dictionary of English, but we also know that *walk* is of relatively common usage, and *perambulate* relatively rare. Similarly, we may know that a structure like *he had been being careful* is possible in English but also that it does not actually occur all that often.

In these examples, we are consciously aware of relative frequency. But in innumerable other cases, we are not. Thus we may know perfectly well that the words *big* and *large* are semantically synonymous, as are the words *little* and *small*, but, if asked, we would not be able to say with any certainty which word in each pair is more frequently used. Nor what other words they tend to keep company with. In the usage of any language there is a tendency for words and structures to co-occur in patterns of relative probability. Some co-occurrences (or **collocations**) are fixed and familiar, as in idiomatic phrases like *to and fro*, *ebb and flow*, *by and large*, *by hook or by crook*, *by fair means or foul*, and so on. Some we know as proverbs: *Too many cooks spoil the broth*, *A rolling stone gathers no moss*, and so on. For the most part, however, we are unaware of the patterning of language in the texts we produce. With the development of corpus linguistics over recent years, such patterning can now be described with great precision.

By means of the computer, linguists can now provide details of the frequency and co-occurrence of words and structures which are simply not accessible to intuition. So they can tell us things about the language we produce that we did not know in the sense that we are not consciously aware of them. But since our usage is informed by these frequencies and patterns of co-occurrence, we must know them in some other subliminal sense and this must be a covert part of our competence in the language. We have

procedural knowledge of them, and what linguistic description can now do is to make this knowledge overt and **declarative**. We shall be considering corpus descriptions in more detail later (Chapter 8).

Hymes identifies the possible, the feasible, the appropriate, and the performed as four distinct aspects of communicative competence, and in the analysis of language in use we can focus attention on any one of them. Given an instance of language, we can, as we have already seen, concern ourselves with how it exemplifies what is formally possible in the language in terms of its encoded grammatical and lexical properties with little if any consideration of any other aspect. If, however, we are interested in the psycholinguistic issue of how these formal properties are actually processed in the mind, then we shall naturally focus attention on feasibility, bringing in the other aspects only to the extent that they are relevant to such processes. A focus on the appropriate will bring context into consideration as a crucial factor in the achievement of pragmatic meaning, and here we are centrally concerned with discourse, as this was earlier defined, with how expressions are assigned a particular reference, force, and effect. As pointed out earlier, this process of meaning making leaves a textual trace, and the patterns of frequency and co-occurrence that this reveals can be independently described without reference to the particular contextual conditions in which the text was produced, or the pragmatic meanings that were achieved in producing them. Here the focus of attention is on the fourth of the Hymes factors, the language that is actually attested as having been performed.

Conclusion

When we use language in the normal circumstances of everyday life, all of these four factors come into play in complex and interdependent ways. But the determining factor is that of contextual appropriateness. It is the discourse we want to achieve that regulates how we draw on the encoded resources of the language to make a text. The language that we produce and process is not designed to demonstrate what is possible or feasible or commonly occurring but to realize a discourse purpose. How then is this done? What exactly does it mean to use language appropriate to context? These are questions that will be taken up in the next chapter.

3
Context

Conditions of language use

We experience language not as something separate but as an intrinsic part of our everyday reality. We do not, in normal circumstances, just display our linguistic knowledge: we put it to use to give shape to our internal thoughts and to give external expression to our communicative purposes. Indeed, we usually find it difficult to display our knowledge in dissociation from these natural conditions of use. So although you might be extremely competent in a particular language, if somebody were to ask you to show your competence by saying something in that language you would in all likelihood be at a loss to know what to say. We only produce language when we have the occasion to use it, and the occasions for use occur in the continuous and changing contexts of our daily life.

Context and shared knowledge

These contexts can be thought of as **situations** in which we find ourselves, the actual circumstances of time and place, the here and now of the home, the school, the work place, and so on. When people talk to each other, they will naturally make reference to what is present in such situations—present in the sense of both place (here) and time (now):

The chalk is over there.
Pass me the tape measure.
There's a page missing.
I like the look of that.
Is that the time?

In these cases, people make sense of what is said by making a connection between the language and the physical context of utterance. *Over there*—on that table by the window. *The tape measure*—the one you have in your hand. *Is that the time?*—five past two, as shown by the clock on the wall, and so on. The language serves to point out something which is present in the perceived environment, and the listener can only understand what the speaker means by the utterance by making the necessary connection. When such utterances are isolated from this shared situation, they have nothing to point to, and so lose their point: *over there* could be anywhere, *the time* could be any time. But being present in the same physical situation is not a guarantee that listeners will make the required connection: they may still fail to identify just what is being indicated (*Over there ... where do you mean?*, *I like the look of that ... the look of what?*). So the context of an utterance cannot simply be the situation in which it occurs but the features of the situation that are taken as relevant. In other words, context is not an external set of circumstances but a selection of them internally represented in the mind.

Context, then, is an abstract representation of a state of affairs. This may be constructed directly from the immediate concrete situation, as in the examples we have considered. But it need not be. It can be entirely independent of such situational factors. Consider again the utterance overheard in a crowded train. The situation, when and where the utterance was actually produced, has no contextual relevance whatever. The context is the common knowledge of the two people concerned, which will have been established in their previous conversation. And it does not matter whether this were to take place in a train, or bus, or in the street, or in a restaurant or anywhere else. Of course, the situation can be contextually relevant. It would be if our conversationalists were to come out with utterances like:

Terribly crowded tonight.
Excuse me, this is my station.

But the point is that the situation is thus *made* contextually relevant. It has no necessary relevance of its own.

Text-activated context

Context, then, is not what is *perceived* in a particular situation, but what is *conceived* as relevant, and situational factors may have no relevance at all. This is particularly clear with written communication, of course. Here there is usually no common situation for the participants to share and so none that can be of any contextual significance. There are exceptions: the exchange of notes between members of an audience for example (*This is a terrible play. Agreed. Let's leave at the interval*), but typically where and when a written text is read is quite different from where and when it was actually produced. Although there can be no appeal to a common situation, however, there must be an appeal to a common context of shared knowledge or otherwise no communication can take place at all. Some of this context will be created by means of the text itself. The following, for example, is the opening paragraph of a magazine article:

> With 300 million native speakers scattered across 20 coun-
> tries, Arabic is the world's sixth largest language. Yet British
> ignorance of and indifference to the Arab world remains start-
> ling: of 737 postgraduate students in Islamic or Middle
> Eastern studies funded by the Economic and Social Research
> Council last year, 12 were British nationals.
> ('Learn among the chickens', Rachel Aspden, *New Statesman*,
> 27 September 2004)

In the opening sentence, the writer provides information to establish the context of shared knowledge. Notice, however, that she assumes that this will activate knowledge that is not made explicit in the text: that the Arab world is to be identified with Islam and the Middle East, for example. Unless such knowledge is activated, the text makes no sense. The same point can be made about the following opening paragraph:

> At the height of the Kosovo crisis in May 1999, Tony Blair was
> on his way to Bucharest, the Romanian capital, to drum up
> local support for NATO's high risk confrontation with Serbia.
> The Prime Minister astonished his advisers by suddenly
> announcing on the aeroplane that he was going to promise

Romania early membership of the European Union in return for its continued backing.

('Europe's very own Puerto Rico', Tom Gallagher, *New Statesman*, 6 September 2004)

Here the writer is apparently unsure that the location of Bucharest is common knowledge, and so helpfully provides the information that it is in Romania. He is more confident that his readers will know who Tony Blair is, so that on the basis of that knowledge will be able to infer that *the Prime Minister* refers to the same person. In the first case, the contextual link is explicitly signalled in the text, and in the second it is not. But there is a good deal more that is assumed to be shared knowledge and so left unsaid: the nature of the Kosovo crisis, for example, and of NATO's confrontation with Serbia, and what these have to do with each other anyway.

The important point to note is that text does not in itself establish context but serves to activate it in the reader's mind. And once activated, it can be extended by inference. Thus in the first of our texts here, it may not be part of a reader's contextual knowledge that the Arab world is to be equated with Islam and the Middle East, but it becomes so by the inference of a connection across two parts of the text. Similarly, when a reader of the second text comes to the expression *on the aeroplane*, the definite article signals that this is something that is assumed to be shared knowledge, so the reader ratifies this assumption by inferring a connection with what has already been said and so infers that Tony Blair was on his way to Bucharest by air, and not, for example, by train.

To summarize the story so far. Context is a psychological construct, a conceptual representation of a state of affairs. In communication, what happens is that a first-person party (a speaker or writer, **P1**) produces a text which keys the second-person party (the listener or reader, **P2**) into a context assumed to be shared. Once the context is keyed in, then it can be extended, or modified, by means of more text: once a degree of contextual convergence is initiated, it provides the conditions for further convergence.

Unshared contexts: illustration from a battlefield

It may be, of course, that the first-person party's assumption of shared context is mistaken, in which case communication falters or breaks down altogether. In spoken interaction, there is usually the possibility of repair whereby the two parties can negotiate the required contextual convergence. This, as we saw earlier, happens when features of the situation are identified as contextually relevant (*Over there ... Where? On the shelf ... Which shelf? ... The bottom one ...* Ah yes, got it). But there can be occasions when a mistaken assumption of shared context cannot be so readily rectified. A particularly striking example of this is provided by an event in British military history.

In October 1854, British and Russian armies met at the battle of Balaclava. During the battle, the British general, Lord Raglan, had positioned himself conveniently on high ground at some distance from the action, and was sending his orders by messengers on horseback to his commanders in the valley below. From this vantage point, he observed a contingent of Russian soldiers retreating with artillery they had captured earlier in the day, and sent an order for his cavalry to intervene. The actual text (written by the general's *aide de camp*) reads as follows:

> Lord Raglan wishes the cavalry to advance rapidly to the front, follow the enemy and try to prevent the enemy carrying away the guns—Troop horse artillery may accompany. French cavalry is on your left. Immediate. R. Airey

The assumption of shared context is very clearly signalled in this text by the use of definite articles: *the cavalry*, *the front*, *the enemy*, *the guns*. What Lord Raglan does not take into account is that his situation up on the heights is different from that of his cavalry commanders down in the valley. They are incapable of seeing what Raglan intends to refer to. Not sharing the same situational vantage point, they are in no position to infer the relevant context that Raglan is presupposing as common knowledge. The only front they can see is one at the end of the valley where the main Russian army is securely entrenched behind their heavy guns. For them, the front is *this* front, the enemy *this* enemy, the guns *these* guns. So they attack in the wrong direction, with disastrous consequences.

The problem with Lord Raglan's text is that it fails as reference. But as was pointed out in the preceding chapter, what writers mean by their texts is not only a matter of what they intend to refer to but also what illocutionary force and perlocutionary effect they intend to achieve. So when Lord Raglan dictates his message, he not only refers to the front and the enemy but in so doing he issues an order. The wording of the text does not make this explicit: *Lord Raglan **wishes** the cavalry ...* But familiar as they are with the conventions of military life, the cavalry commanders know full well that their general is not just expressing a wish but that his message has the force of an order which they cannot choose but to obey promptly, particularly in the context of the battlefield. As to the effect of the message, the result that Lord Raglan intended was to engage his cavalry in a relatively minor action. The effect of its interpretation, however, was quite different and the result was a catastrophe.

In the case of this calamity, communication breaks down because the second-person parties, the cavalry commanders down in the valley, are quite literally not in a position, situationally, to key into the context presupposed by the first person, the general up on the heights. More commonly, however, difficulties occur when the first person presupposes preconceived knowledge of the world that the second person does not share. Thus our understanding of the text extract cited earlier about Tony Blair and Romania depends on our knowing about the Kosovo crisis. The article from which it is taken appears in a current affairs magazine and its writer assumes, reasonably enough, that its readers will be informed about the world events the magazine is, of its nature, concerned with. The point to be noted here is that generally speaking all texts are recipient-designed in one way or another so that if you are not the recipient who is, so to speak, designated, you are likely to have problems keying into the context that the text producer presupposes. This is obvious enough when we encounter texts dealing in specialist subjects we are unfamiliar with—in genetics, for example (in my own particular case), animal husbandry, nuclear physics. But it is important to note that all texts, whether deemed to be specialist or not, are designed with preconceived ideas about what can be counted on as common insider knowledge in the particular groups of recipients they are produced for. If you are an outsider, you are obviously likely to have difficulties making the necessary contextual connections.

Context and shared values

Context can be thought of as knowledge of the world that a text is used to refer to, but of the world as it is known by particular groups of people. And this has not only to do with what these different groups know about as matters of fact (and others do not), but also with their distinctive way of thinking about these things. In the extract we considered earlier, for example, the writer does not only take it for granted that the reader will know about the connection between the Arab world and Islam, which is a matter of fact, but also that the reader will share his point of view about the state of affairs that he describes and so accept the force of what he is saying. Thus, the expression *British ignorance of and indifference to the Arab world remains startling* is not a statement of objective fact but the assertion of opinion, and one that the writer assumes the reader will accept. Appeal is made here not to shared knowledge but to shared values. The same point can be made about features of the second extract about Tony Blair: *drum up* (rather than *get* or *obtain* or *canvass*), *local support*, *high-risk confrontation* are expressions which seem to suggest disapproval, and again the reader is invited to adopt the same attitude, to share the same **position** or point of view, and so to ratify these remarks not as the statement of objective information, but as critical comment. Consider another text from the same source:

> After stealing the Tories' policies, New Labour has inevitably gone on to steal the Tories' wives. But that the wife should be Kimberly Fortier, publisher of the *Spectator,* seems surprising. Isn't that magazine the enemy of those who undermine the family? Alas, no: it may get its politics from the *Telegraph*, but it now gets its morals from the *Daily Sport* …
> (*New Statesman*, 23 August 2004)

Here it is assumed that the reader is already in the know about what is mentioned here: not only about the particular recent events involving wife-stealing and Kimberly Fortier, but more generally about the more permanent background against which these events take place: the politics of the Tories and New Labour, and the nature of the three publications that are mentioned. But it is also assumed that the reader will accept the subjective way these events and their background have been represented here, recognize that this text is intended to have the force of ridicule and the effect of amused contempt.

Conclusion

The contexts that texts, whether spoken or written, are designed to key into are constructs of reality as conceived by particular groups of people, representations of what they know of the world and how they think about it. Although, as we have seen, some of the knowledge that the text producer assumes to be shared is of particular things, events, persons, either within the immediate situation of utterance or not, these particulars are typically related to more general schematic structures of knowledge. Thus it is assumed in the text we have just been considering that the particular mention of wife-stealing and Kimberly Fortier will be related to the more general **schema** of British politics, and the mention of Tony Blair and his astonishing announcement in the text cited earlier will be related to the more general schemata of the Kosovo crisis and of the European Union and its affairs. If readers cannot ratify these assumptions, they will be at a loss to know what discourse the writers intend to mean by their texts in terms of their reference, force, and effect.

Of course, even if the receivers of texts are contextually in the know and *are* in a position to ratify the intentions of the text producers, they may fail to engage this knowledge for one reason or another. Communication is not simply a matter of bringing kinds of knowledge into correspondence, but of bringing them into a degree of convergence, and this may call for quite complex negotiation. We will take up what this involves in Chapter 6. But meanwhile, we need to take a closer look at how kinds of contextual knowledge are conventionally structured. We need to explore the concept of the schema.

4

Schematic conventions

Context and situation

As we have seen in the previous chapter, language use is a matter of constructing and construing texts by keying them into contexts so as to realize discourse meaning, that is to say, the message in the mind as intended by the text producer on the one hand, and as interpreted by the text receiver on the other.

As was pointed out earlier, context is an abstract representation, a mental construct. It may be abstracted from the immediate situation of utterance, as when reference is made to something that is directly perceptible by both parties in an interaction. So if somebody asks me to close the door, for example, I can readily infer that what is being referred to is a particular door in the room we are in. This is a case of what is called **deixis**—the pointing out of something immediately and perceptibly present in the situation of utterance: that door there, this door here.

But context is obviously not confined to what is situationally present in the here and now. The language we produce or receive in the process of communication does not come unexpectedly out of the blue. It is part of the continuity of our individual and social lives, and so always related to the context in our heads of what we know and believe. This context in the head is what was referred to in the preceding chapter as schematic structures of knowledge, and it is this that we engage to make sense of language, when we realize discourse from the text.

The concept of the schema

A **schema** is a construct of familiar knowledge. How it works is best illustrated by reference to the work of the psychologist F. C. Bartlett, who introduced the concept over 70 years ago in a book called *Remembering*, to account for the findings of certain experiments he carried out. In one of his experiments a group of British students were asked to read a North American Indian story called *The War of the Ghosts* and then rewrite it from memory as accurately as possible. What they did in their versions of the story was to change the events so that they corresponded more closely with their own conventional and customary reality, very different from that represented in the original. In other words, the discourse they derived from the text was one that suited their preconceived schematic expectations.

The text that these students were asked to read and retell came, of course, from a culture very different from their own, and we can describe the disparity between the original story and their versions of as an instance of cross-cultural misunderstanding. To the extent that schematic assumptions are socially shared by a particular community, we can say that they are indeed cultural constructs. But we also have to allow for what is familiar and customary and expected, and so schematically shared, among smaller groups of people—professional and family groups, for example, who we would not normally speak of as sharing a culture. The process of making sense by taking schematic bearings applies to the interpretation of all texts. You cannot make sense of anything without bringing it within the confines of what is preconceived as familiar. Everything new has to be related to what is given. But it is, of course, a matter of degree: sometimes it is relatively easy to accommodate new information into existing schemata, sometimes (as in *The War of the Ghosts*) relatively difficult, but some accommodation needs always to be made.

Frames of reference

What happens in text interpretation is that the language triggers off the recall of some familiar state of affairs, some schema or other, and this sets up an expectation of what is to follow.

Here, to take a simple example, is the first sentence of an article from a recent edition of a British news magazine:

In the past it took a disaster to bring the Olympics to London.

The language here activates schematic knowledge about the Olympic games and how different cities bid to host them every four years. So it indicates a **frame of reference** and at the same time projects the reader's attention forward to what is to come next. Readers anticipate that they are to be told more about previous occasions when the Olympic games were held in London. Sure enough, the text continues as follows:

In 1908 the city stepped in after Vesuvius erupted, leaving Rome bereft. In 1948 it was called upon to rescue the Olympic ideal for a Europe ravaged by fascist dictatorship.

Again, readers can only understand all this about London rescuing the Olympic ideal if they can call up the frame of reference of the Second World War in Europe.

This process of keying the language into an appropriate frame of reference to make sense of text comes so naturally to us that we take it for granted, and it is easy to suppose that the meaning is actually in the text itself and not derived from it by this kind of schematic inference. But it is not difficult to demonstrate how much our interpretation depends upon it.

Suppose, for example, you overheard the following remark:

The service left much to be desired.

Now if you look up the word 'service' in a dictionary you will find that it has several semantic meanings (religious ceremony, public assistance, set of crockery, and so on). The question is which of them is pragmatically appropriate in this text, and the answer is that we cannot tell. We lack a frame of reference, and so we cannot anticipate what is to come next. But if we were to modify the text a little:

The service last Sunday left much to be desired.

Now we would tend to interpret the word as meaning a *church* service because in our familiar world such services are customarily held on Sundays. And once the church service schema is invoked, then we would anticipate that what follows would fit into that frame of reference:

> The service last Sunday left much to be desired. The hymns were badly chosen, the prayers inappropriate, and the sermon too long. And what is more, the organ was too loud.

Notice that once a frame of reference is established, the use of definite articles becomes appropriate ('*the* hymns,' '*the* prayers', and so on) because the phases refer to what is common schematic knowledge: a church service conventionally includes prayers, hymns, a sermon, and there is a choir, an organ, and so on.

Of course readers can be mistaken and invoke the wrong frame of reference. They can be deliberately misled and their expectations thwarted. We might, for example, extend our text in different ways:

> The service last Sunday left much to be desired. Most of the staff had taken the day off, and we had to wait ages between courses.

Or:

> The service last Sunday left much to be desired. So we lost the game.

Having been induced at the beginning of the text to think of a church service, readers now have to shift the frame of reference and adjust their expectations.

But it is possible (if you are feeling perverse enough) to compose a text which frustrates this shift and adjustment because it continues to be relatable to two quite different possible frames of reference at the same time. Consider the following:

> Rocky slowly got up from the mat, planning his escape. He hesitated a moment and thought. Things were not going well. What bothered him most was being held, especially since the charge against him had been weak. He considered his present situation. The lock that held him was strong, but he thought he could break it.

What is being described here? The text is ambiguous in that it admits of two interpretations. If we take 'Rocky' as referring to a prisoner, then what we have here are his thoughts about escaping from his cell. In this case, we might propose extending the text by adding:

But he would have to wait until the warder had finished his rounds.

We could, however, take 'Rocky' to refer not to a prisoner but to a wrestler and then what we have are his thoughts about how to get the better of his opponent. In this a quite different textual extension would be schematically suitable:

Then the bell rang for the end of the round.

The ambiguity of the text here is sustained by the use of words which call up two possible and competing frames of reference. As mentioned earlier, word forms frequently encode more than one semantic meaning and these are recorded in a dictionary. When put to pragmatic use, words function as schema activators, but of course they are not usually on their own: they connect with other words in a text, and the connection will usually have the effect of directing the reader's attention to just one schema by elimination. Thus readers connect the words *hymn* and *prayer* with *service* to project a church schema and all other semantic meanings of the word are discarded. In the case of ambiguity, readers do not know what to eliminate and they have to keep more than one possible schema in mind at one and the same time.

Of course, in reference to the text about Rocky, if you know nothing about wrestling, there will be no wrestling schema to invoke, and words like *escape* and *lock* are then likely to bring only prisons to mind. Similarly, the words *hymn*, *prayer*, *sermon*, and so on will only call to mind a religious service if these things are customary in the kind of religious service you know about. Schemata are representations in the mind of what is familiar or customary. But all this is relative: what is familiar to one group of people may be unknown to another, and customs vary across communities. So what such schemata represent are culturally different ways of ordering the world, different versions of social reality.

Frames and cultural assumptions

These schemata are cultural, taken-for-granted constructs, and they become so firmly entrenched in our consciousness that we often find it difficult to envisage any alternative ways of thinking. We talk about common sense but tend to forget that this sense is only locally common and is in fact communal sense—the way a particular community has constructed reality for itself. As with Bartlett's subjects, when we encounter a text that does not fit our culturally schematized world, we naturally find it hard to make sense of it. Consider the following often cited example:

> A man was taking a walk with his son one day and as they were crossing the road, a car came round a corner unexpectedly and hit the boy, injuring him badly. An ambulance was called for and the boy was taken to the nearest hospital and into the operating theatre. On seeing the boy, the surgeon suddenly let out a cry of horror: 'My God this is my son!'

Anybody who reads this text for the first time may well be mystified by it. How can it be that the surgeon suddenly recognizes his son at the hospital, when he was with the boy earlier at the time of the accident—and anyway how can the father be out walking with his son and working at the hospital at the same time? It seems that we have a mystery here that we need a Sherlock Holmes to solve. But the mystery only comes about because of our preconceived schematic assumptions and is easy enough to dispel. Suppose the surgeon is a woman. As soon as that possibility is suggested, then the mystery disappears. By the same token, if we were to change the text by replacing the word *surgeon* with *nurse*, there is no mystery at all. Elementary, my dear Watson, as Sherlock Holmes might say (and in writing this, I am aware that I too am assuming cultural knowledge my reader might not share!).

The idea that the surgeon is a woman does not (for many people at least) come immediately to mind is because the mind is naturally inclined to interpret things by relating them to what is schematically established as normal and customary. A reader with different schematic expectations, someone living in a society where it is common for surgeons to be women (and nurses, say, men), would not find this text mysterious in the least. But notice that once the possibility of the surgeon being a woman is proposed, this is readily recognized as solving the mystery, and it all seems so obvious—'Of course', people usually say, 'why didn't I think of that?' So it is not that the idea of a woman surgeon is difficult to entertain. It is simply that it is less directly accessible.

What schemata do is to provide us with a convenient framework for understanding. Without them we would be at a loss to make sense of any text, or indeed to make sense of any of the circumstances of everyday life. At the same time they have their disadvantages in that they can impose a preconceived pattern on things and impede us from recognizing any alternative concept of reality. The danger is that once a text has triggered off a particular schema, the reader may interpret what follows in reference to it and disregard anything in the text that does not sustain it. As we have seen, a particular schematic projection, then, can override textual signals that would allow the engagement of a different schema. This accounts for the lack of convergence, mentioned previously, between the discourse that is interpreted (what the text means to the reader or listener) and the discourse that is intended (what a writer or speaker means by a text).

Interpersonal routines

So far we have been talking about schemata as frames of reference, as **ideational** constructs, that is to say, as shared conceptions of a third-person reality—the reality out there. As such they represent what a group, large or small, consider to be customary, normal, natural ways of thinking about events. But there are also schematic constructs of a different kind. These represent not the customary ways in which we conceive of the third-person world, but customary ways in which we engage with second persons, the conventions we take for granted that concern how people normally interact with each other. These we can refer to as **interpersonal schemata**.

Examples of such schemata would be those that inform the everyday routines we follow when meeting or greeting people, or the different transactions we carry out in **service encounters**—buying a train ticket, checking in at a hotel, making enquiries over the phone, and so on. The customary ways of doing these things are so familiar to us that we take them for granted, until we discover, sometimes to our discomfiture, that they do not always apply and that other people, from different cultures or social groups, follow rather different schematic conventions of behaviour. Consider the routine of introduction and first meeting. The following three move pattern might be taken as typical.

A *Introduction*: Tom, this is Jane
B (Tom) *Greeting*: How do you do?
C (Jane) *Greeting*: How do you do?

There are, however, all kinds of variations that might occur in the actual wording of these moves. The introduction might be formally expressed as *Tom, may I introduce you to Jane*, or informally as *Tom—Jane*, depending on the occasion or the people involved. These factors are also likely to affect which **terms of address** are used for the first person mentioned (*Mr Jones, Professor Jones, Sir Tom Jones*) and which terms of reference for the second (may I introduce *Jane Grey, Mrs Grey, Lady Jane Grey*). There may be conventions about which of the two people is to be the referent and which the addressee. According to one code of etiquette, the man should always be the referent and always introduced to the woman as addressee, and not the other way round, so the introduction move in our example should really be formulated as *Jane, this is Tom* or *Jane, may I introduce you to Tom*. For other people, the order is a matter of indifference—it is not in their schema for this particular routine.

Turning now to the two greetings moves, these two might be differently expressed as, for example, *How are you? How are you doing? Nice to meet you*, or quite simply, and very informally, *Hi*. These might be in free variation, so that it does not matter which expression is used. But again it could be that factors like the kind of social occasion, or the status of the people being introduced would customarily require one form of wording rather than another. So in some situations, the use of *How do you do* or *Hi* would be considered out of place, marked as not conforming to customary practice. We might note, too, that although the greetings in our example take the linguistic form of interrogative sentences, they do not function pragmatically as questions in this routine: the first greeting does not call for an answer, and if one were to be given, like *I am doing very well thank you*, this would be unexpected and rather odd. We might also note that in the rather different routine customarily used for greeting people you know already, it was be equally odd to use the expression *How do you do*, though *Hi*, with or without *How are you*, would be appropriate—appropriate, that is to say, in some communities on some occasions.

When these different schematic conventions for appropriate interpersonal behaviour are described in detail in this way, it makes them seem complicated—perhaps absurdly so. But people do not generally experience them as complicated because they acquire them quite naturally as part of the process of being socialized into the accepted ways of behaving in the social groups they belong to. It is when we find ourselves in situations where the interpersonal routines are different from those we have become accustomed to that difficulties arise. Take the example of Eliza Doolittle in George Bernard Shaw's play *Pygmalion* (made familiar by the musical version, *My Fair Lady*). Eliza is a cockney flower girl who Professor Higgins sets out to train to converse like people in a higher social class. This (slightly abridged) is the scene where she tries out her newly acquired polite routine for the first time:

MRS EYNSFORD HILL (*introducing*) My daughter Clara.
LIZA How do you do?
CLARA How do you do? ...
FREDDY I've certainly had the pleasure.
MRS EYNSFORD HILL My son Freddy.
LIZA How do you do?
(*a long and painful pause ensues*)
MRS HIGGINS (*at last, conversationally*) Will it rain, do you think?
LIZA The shallow depression to the west of these islands is likely to move slowly in an easterly direction. There are no indications of any great change in the barometrical situation.
FREDDY Ha! ha! how awfully funny.
LIZA What is wrong with that, young man. I bet I got it right.
(*Pygmalion*, Act 3)

Liza did get the language right in that she made no mistakes in her grammar and pronunciation. What is wrong with her utterance is that it does not conform to the convention that the mention of weather is only a ploy to get a conversation going. Liza, unaware of this, produces a totally inappropriate and unexpected reply and does not understand why Freddy finds it funny. For his part, Freddy would naturally assume she knows the convention and so is deliberately flouting it in order to be amusing.

The point to be made is that what we take for granted as 'ordinary' or 'normal' behaviour actually presupposes a mutual understanding of quite complex schematic conventions. And we have only been discussing how these regulate the language we use. But we must remember that these utterances we have been considering, these introductions and greetings, are kinds of social action and are accompanied by other conventions that define appropriate behaviour. We have already mentioned one of these, namely which of the two people being introduced is to be the addressee, and which the referent. This might depend on sex, or on age, or on social status. Another convention has to do with accompanying physical action—do you shake hands or not, do the people being introduced look at each other? Another convention concerns proximity—how close do people stand to each other, not only when they meet and greet but when they engage in conversation more generally?

Adjacency pairs

The apparently very simple routine we have been considering is only one of numerous sets of schematic conventions that regulate interpersonal behaviour. Whenever we engage in interaction with other people we bring with us expectations about customary procedures. Thus in a conversation, the participants assume that they will take turns to speak and that there will be conventional signals that indicate when it is time to take a turn, and what kind of turn is expected. So in the example we considered earlier, Tom recognizes that A has completed a turn and knows that it is time for his turn, and knows too that the kind of turn he needs to produce is a greeting. Similarly, Jane recognizes that it is now her turn and that she is required to produce a reciprocal greeting. If they failed to take up their expected turns, it would be noticed as a marked departure from the normal routine.

A greeting, whether following an introduction (as in our example) or not, conventionally requires a greeting in return. The two turns make up a minimal routine which has been called an **adjacency pair**. Another example would be question and answer turns. The asking of a question will generally signal a shift of turn and require that the turn should take the form of a reply. What kind of reply is appropriate will, of course, depend on the kind of question, and in some cases this dependency is also a matter of conventional routine. When A asks a question of B, it will be, more often than not, in order to elicit something that B knows about but A does not. If A is a teacher, however, and B a pupil the question is likely to be about something A already knows about, its purpose being to get the pupil to display their knowledge in an approved way. As every pupil knows, there are penalties for not conforming to this particular routine. Similarly, questions asked in a cross-examination in court are of a particular kind and are designed to elicit particular kinds of answer. In both classrooms and courtrooms, the dependency between the question/answer adjacency pair is exploited to constrain and control. This brings up the question of how people use routines to exercise power—a question we shall be taking up in more detail later (in Chapter 6).

So far we have been looking at the adjacency pairs greeting/greeting and question/answer separately, but they can also combine as sub-routines in, for example, service encounters like

A (shop assistant): Good morning. Can I help you?
B (customer): Good morning. I am looking for …
A (hotel receptionist): Good morning. Can I help you?
B (guest): Good morning. I have a reservation.
A Name?
B Smith

Here we have routine patterns in a single turn, as we do in what has become quite common as a waiter's self-introduction in a restaurant:

Good evening. How are you doing? My name is Martin. I am your waiter for the evening. Are you ready to order?

Or the reply we get when we make enquiries at a telephone call centre:

Good morning. My name is Linda. How can I help you?

Typically in these cases, the greeting, introduction, and question occur in this fixed sequence and without a pause to allow for a shift of turn. It would be an unconventional departure from the routine for the addressee to take up a reciprocal turn and take the greeting and introduction at their face value:

WAITER Good evening. How are you doing? My name is Martin.
CUSTOMER Nice to meet you. I am doing very well, thank you. My name is Ronald, and this is my wife, Audrey …

CALL CENTRE OPERATOR Good morning. My name is Linda.
CALLER How do you do. My name is Ronald.

In these waiter and call centre examples, the token greeting (combined with the self introduction) is an obligatory part of a standard one-turn routine. In other service encounters, greetings may be optional. At a busy ticket counter in a railway station, for example, they might be dispensed with so as to carry out the transaction more briskly:

A *(traveller)*: Return to Brighton, please.
B *(ticket seller)*: Thirty pounds.
A Thanks.

Genres

The interpersonal schemata we have been looking at so far are those which find expression in the regular routines of everyday spoken interactions. Although, as has been noted, they represent socio-cultural knowledge of a subtle kind, they are relatively simple in structure, consisting as they do of a few turns at talk. But there are also interpersonal schemata which are much more extensive. So it is that we recognize certain stretches of interaction as **speech events** of specific kinds, or **genres**, and we have names to attach to them: meeting, interview, cross-examination, debate, and so on. Here again there are procedures which those involved are assumed to be familiar with and are expected to conform to. A committee meeting of a formal kind, for example, follows a certain agenda which specifies the order of business, with a chairperson who sees to it that the order is respected, and who controls how discussion proceeds by nominating those who are to take turns at talk, even requiring them to address what they say to the chair rather than to other people present. Those who depart from the established procedure are said to be speaking 'out of turn' or to be 'out of order'. Not all meetings, and certainly not all other kinds of genre, are as ritualistic or schematically rigid as this, of course, but there will always be a set of assumptions and expectations about what behaviour is appropriate to the genre, about what is the 'done thing' and what is not.

The kinds of genre referred to so far—meeting, interview, debate, and so on—are all speech events which involve turn taking. There are others which do not: speeches, for example, or sermons (in one tradition at least), which consist of only one, long (sometimes all too long) turn. Here, obviously, the kind of communication cannot be defined by reference to schematic assumptions about the appropriate way of participating in an exchange, for there is no exchange. But although there is no participation, this does not mean that there is no engagement. It is indeed the purpose of the politician on the podium, the priest in the pulpit, to get the listeners interpersonally engaged, and the speaker designs what they have to say to that end. And the listeners know what to expect and respond accordingly. They know well enough what is likely to be referred to and what kind of communicative force and effect the speakers intend to achieve by what they say. So, the schematic pattern here is not that of directly interactive turn taking, as with the introductions, greetings, and service encounters we considered earlier in this chapter, but of kinds of illocutionary act and their intended effect as were discussed in Chapter 2.

Speeches and sermons are examples of speech events which are single-turn genres. The most obvious examples of single-turn genres, however, are those of written language use. Although there are times when the interactants overtly participate in written communication (in an exchange of notes, for example, or email messages), written texts, as was pointed out in Chapter 1, are generally not jointly produced in the process of interaction. Nevertheless, here, too, there is obviously interpersonal involvement. The writer seeks to engage the reader and does so by making appeal to the conventions that define particular genres which are assumed to be common knowledge. So if I open up my newspaper to read a football report, or look up a menu in a cookery book, or consult a manual of instructions for assembling equipment, I will have some idea of what to expect because I know how football reports, menus, and instructions are typically written. Or, if I venture into writing myself and decide to offer an article to a learned journal, reporting on a piece of research, I know that I will be expected to structure it in conformity to the genre which has been established by the **discourse community** of scholars in this area of learning as appropriate for this kind of written communication. This might require me to begin by locating my own study in the context of current research in the field, to follow a certain format in describing the design of my investigation, to present my findings in a certain way, and so on. Compliance with such requirements can be seen as a condition of membership of this particular discourse community, and of publication in this particular journal.

Conclusion

How strict the compliance has to be will vary, of course. Genre conventions are by no means rigidly fixed and always adhered to: they are naturally subject to variation and change because there will always be some room for individual manoeuvre. People will have schematic knowledge of what is typical of particular genres and this will prime their expectations. But these expectations may need to be subsequently adjusted. The ideational and interpersonal schemata we have been considering in this chapter are relatively stable knowledge structures or states of mind, customized or conventionalized as normal in a particular community. But we also need to consider how they are put to work, made operational in the production of actual text. This is the concern of the next chapter.

5
Co-textual relations

Information structure

As was pointed out earlier (in Chapter 2), one of the things we do when we use language is to formulate a proposition, to make reference to some state of affairs. Let us suppose that we want to express a proposition about a certain event, a demonstration, for example, and the actions of the police in dispersing the crowd. English allows for the possibility of expressing our proposition in different ways, for example:

The police dispersed the demonstrators.
The demonstrators were dispersed by the police.

If we think of these as linguistic forms, we recognize the first as an active and the second as a passive sentence with *the police* being the subject in the first case and *the demonstrators* in the second. But if we think of these expressions as utterances, they are textual variants, different ways of distributing the propositional information. In terms of textual structure, the first piece of information, which here takes the form of a subject noun phrase, is said to be the **theme**, and the rest of the utterance the **rheme**. But what if we want to go on and say something else? How would we order the information in the next utterance? We could follow the same pattern and start with the same theme (T):

The police(T) dispersed the demonstrators. Some of the law officers(T) …

Or we might reverse the order and thematize the previous rheme (R):

The police(T) dispersed the demonstrators(R). The banners they were carrying(R→T) …

Or we could, of course, introduce a different theme altogether:

The police(T1) dispersed the crowd. The motorcade(T2) …

It needs to be noticed, however, that whether a theme is different or not is by no means easy to determine. It may be a matter of simply identifying a semantic connection (recognizing *police* and *law officers* as synonymous, for example), but schematic knowledge may also be involved. There is, for example, no semantic link between the words *demonstrator* and *banner*: to recognize the thematic connection here, you need to invoke what you know about demonstrations.

The alternative thematizations we have been considering are brought about by changes in grammatical structure, and the use of active and passive forms is only one way of signalling theme and rheme. There are other possibilities, for example the use of sentences like:

What the police did(T) was to disperse the demonstrators.

But thematization can also be brought about by changing the sequence of constituents in a sentence without affecting its structure, as in:

The police(T) dispersed the demonstrators early in the day.
Early in the day(T), the police dispersed the demonstrators.

English, then, in common with other languages, makes provision within its encoding conventions for expressing propositional meaning in different ways. The question arises as to why the users of the language would want to take advantage of this provision. Theme and rheme can be easily identified as a feature of text, but what is it that motivates the use of one textual variant rather than another? What communicative intention lies behind them: in other words, what might their discourse function be? Here things are not so easy.

An item of information might be given the status of theme because the first-person text producer, **P1**, assumes it to be **given**, that is to say, already known by the second-person receiver, **P2**. In this case, the theme simply confirms common knowledge and sets the scene for the **new** information to be provided in the rheme. Conversely, the theme could signal the main **topic** that P1 wants to talk about, with the rheme representing **comment** on that topic. P1's use of the theme/rheme sequence to signal given/new information is clearly P2-oriented and co-operative: it expresses, we might say, consideration of P2's position (*Let me remind you of what you know already* …). But the use of theme/rheme to signal topic/comment is quite different. This is P1-oriented, with P1 asserting his/her own position (*This is what I am going to talk about* …).

It is clear that thematization plays a crucial role in organizing information in a text. What its significance is for discourse interpretation in particular instances, however, is not so clear, as we shall see when we return to it later, in Chapter 7.

Text linkage

Theme/rheme assignment is a general way of organizing information and carrying reference over from one proposition to the next. But the linking of theme and rheme across parts of text depends on the identification of other more specific and small-scale connections to establish text continuity. As communication takes place, in speech or writing, what is said at a particular point naturally makes reference to what has been said before and a context is created in the mind and signalled in the text in the process of its production. We saw this earlier in the passage about Tony Blair and Kosovo. The writer assumes that what is mentioned at the beginning will be kept in mind and serve as a context for what follows:

> *Tony Blair* was on his way to Bucharest …. *The Prime Minister* astonished his advisers …

Here the definite article signals shared knowledge and prompts the reader to refer back to a previous mention that can be connected with it. Further linkage is provided later by the use of a pronoun:

> … by suddenly announcing that *he* was going to drum up local support …

The pronoun, as its name suggests, acts as a **pro-form**, that is to say, it stands in for the fuller expression that precedes it. This kind of text-internal, or **co-textual** connection is known as **anaphora**.

Anaphora and pro-forms

It should be noted that this anaphoric connection is not directly signalled by the linguistic pro-forms themselves. It has to be inferred by identifying and interpreting the cross-reference. Take the pronoun *he*. This encodes the semantic features of singular and masculine and it works anaphorically only if these features can be traced back to realize a reference in common with a previous mention. In the present case, this is easy to do because there is only one possible candidate: *he* is identified as having a referential link to *The Prime Minister* and *Tony Blair*. But there might be, and indeed quite commonly is, more than one possible candidate for referential connection. Consider another pronoun, *its*, as it occurs in the second part of our text:

> The Prime Minister astonished his advisers by suddenly announcing on the aeroplane that he was going to promise Romania early membership of the European Union in return for *its* continued backing.

Its encodes the semantic features of singular and non-human and these features are to be found in *Romania*, *the European Union*, and even in *membership of the European Union*, so it could be linked linguistically to any of these three. The appropriate anaphoric connection is a matter of inferring which makes most sense pragmatically, which corresponds most closely with the reader's contextual knowledge of the world—in other words, it is a matter of discourse interpretation. The writer here assumes that such contextual knowledge will indeed be activated, but if in doubt, he could, of course, have made this correspondence more textually explicit by simply repeating the previous mention:

> … in return for *Romania's* continued backing.

Or copying more **semantic features** from the previous mention in a more explicit pro-form as in:

> … in return for *that country's* continued backing.

We return here to the points made in Chapter 2 about feasibility. For in making intended meaning more evident by a more explicit pro-form, the writer makes it easier to process.

There are occasions, of course, when writers would have been better advised to avoid minimal pro-forms and provide more explicit textualization of their discourse intentions to increase feasibility and avoid misunderstanding, or unintended ambiguity. Consider the following text:

> Unfortunately in the weeks to come autumn leaves will create a dangerous hazard, especially to the elderly when they fall and become a soggy mess on the pavement.

Here the pronoun *they* copies only the semantic feature of plurality (unlike the singular pronouns, *he*, *she*, *it*, the plural is not marked for gender in English). There are two plural noun phrases in the text which are linguistic candidates for co-textual linkage: *autumn leaves* and *the elderly*. The intended anaphoric connection (one must suppose) is between *they* and *autumn leaves*. But an alternative interpretation is possible, of course by calling up a fanciful context which sets up an anaphoric connection with the pronoun and *the elderly,* so that it is they who fall and become a soggy mess on the pavement. Hence the comic effect.

Cohesion

The identification of connections that are linguistically signalled, like those between a pronoun and a previous noun phrase, enables us to recognize the **cohesion** of a text. But the personal pronouns we have been considering so far are only one kind of cohesive device. There are many others. Features of a preceding noun phrase can also be copied by pro-forms that consist of nouns of more general or inclusive meaning as when, in the example given earlier, there is a cohesive link between *Romania* and *that country*. We might note that the expression *that country* does not actually refer here to the country itself as a geographical location, but is shorthand for *the government of that country*. That being so, an expression like *its government* or *the government* would also serve as a pro-form to make the cohesive link in this passage. If, however, the word *Romania* were to be used in reference to the country itself, then a different expression would be called for. Consider the following interaction:

A We went to Romania last summer. Beautiful *country*. We loved *the place*.
B Really? We were *there* a year or two ago—didn't think much of *it*.

As we can see here, cohesive pro-forms vary in how much meaning is copied from the previous mention: the very general noun *place* copies less than the more particular noun *country*, but copies more than the pronoun *it*.

But cohesion does not only involve the kind of noun phrase or nominal replacement we have been considering so far. In this exchange, for example, the adverb *there* is clearly a pro-form that links up with the preceding *Romania, country, place*. But what it copies is the concept of location as would be expressed in prepositional phrases like *to Romania* or *in Romania*. And verb phrases can be copied into pro-forms and connected in a similar way. Consider the following:

A We went to Romania for our holidays last summer.
B We *did* too.
A We thought it was a wonderful place.
B Well, we *didn't*.

Here the verb form *did*, simply copies the features of action and past time to make the required cohesive link with the preceding verb phrase. Again, alternatives are available to make the link more explicit if necessary, as in

We were *there then* too.
So did we.
We *did the same*.
Well, we *didn't think so*.

These **cohesive devices**, then, serve to link parts of a text together. It is important to note, however, that they (i.e. these cohesive devices) do so (i.e. link parts of the texts together) so that new content is understood in relation to the context that has been established in the reader's mind by what has been said before.

That is to say, the text design has a discourse function—it is designed to key into context so as to express the message the producer has in mind.

So far we have been considering cohesive pro-forms that have an **anaphoric** function, that is to say, that work retrospectively in that they copy features from preceding expressions in a text. But we should note that pro-forms can also work prospectively as **cataphoric** devices, that is to say they can precede a more explicit mention. Thus, to take a simple example, the pronoun *he* functions anaphorically in:

When the Prime Minister was on his way to Romania, ←*he* astonished his advisers.

But it functions as a cataphoric pro-form in:

When *he*→ was on his way to Romania, the Prime Minister astonished his advisers.

Cohesion and the least effort principle

It needs to be stressed that pro-forms, whether functioning anaphorically or cataphorically, are tokens of meaning which only make sense when their relationship with what has preceded or what follows, is both identified and interpreted. This, as we have seen with cases of ambiguity, is not always successfully achieved. This might lead one to wonder why language users do not always make use of semantically fuller expressions to ensure a more explicit cohesive connection. The difficulty is that this can result in a reduction of feasibility by getting readers to process information they do not need. The general point here is that communication generally operates on a least effort principle and we only use as much language as we need to make the required contextual connection. The problem is always to know how to regulate the degree of co-textual explicitness by the judicial choice of pro-form. How much do writers need to spell out cohesive links, how far can they count on readers making sense of the text without them? Consider, for example, the following newspaper text.

The Muslim Council of Britain has set up an investigation into mosques, women's organizations and Islamic youth centres across the country to root out extremism.

Sir Iqbal Sacranie, secretary general of the council, told The Independent that the council, which has more than 400 affliliates and is the most powerful Muslim body in the country of Britain, has set up the focus groups to locate and combat the terrorist threat. Its early findings will be revealed in a national conference in September, he said.

The move comes amid allegations that the council is failing mainstream Muslims and has its roots in extremist politics. (*Independent*, online edition, 15 August 2005)

The use of the definite article in *the country* in the first and second paragraphs here, and *the council* in the second signals that we are meant to connect these expressions anaphorically to what has preceded—to *Britain* in the first case, and to *The Muslim Council of Britain* in the second. Similarly, the pronoun *he* links anaphorically to *Sir Iqbal Sacranie*. These connections are easy enough to make and it would seem perverse to spell them out. To do so (i.e. to spell such connections, i.e. the connections between *country* and *Britain* and between *the council* and *the Muslim Council of Britain* and between *he* and *Sir Iqbal Sacranie* ...) would, as is plain to see, make the text unnecessarily cumbersome:

> Sir Iqbal Sacranie, secretary general of the Muslim Council of Britain, told The Independent that the Muslim Council of Britain, which has more than 400 affliliates and is the most powerful Muslim body in the country of Britain ...

However, the definite reference *the focus groups* is rather less straightforward. There is no preceding noun *groups*, nor any noun which can be related semantically to it. In this case, what we have to do is assume that the co-textual verb phrase *has set up* signals that *the focus groups* and *an investigation* are intended to be synonymous so that what is being referred to is the investigation mentioned in the first paragraph. Here we could argue that a more explicit co-textual link would be desirable. A similar point might be made about the anaphoric pronoun *its*.

Being singular there is no cohesion here with the plural noun phrase *the focus groups* so it is presumably meant to make a connection with *an investigation into mosques, women's organizations* … (and not to *The Muslim Council of Britain*). We could make the text more cohesive, therefore, by rewriting it as follows:

> [The council] has set up the focus groups of the investigation to locate and combat the terrorist threat. The early findings of this investigation will be revealed in a national conference in September, Sir Iqbal Sacranie said.

Or, if we wanted to relate the reference to focus groups more explicitly to the three areas of investigation mentioned in the first paragraph (and which are presumably to be focused on), we might rewrite the text along the following lines:

> [The council] has set up groups to focus investigation on mosques, women's organizations, and Islamic youth centres in order to locate and combat the terrorist threat.

An alternative way of doing this would be to provide a lexical connection in the first paragraph by using the word *focus*. For example:

> The Muslim Council of Britain has set up an investigation which will focus attention on mosques, women's organizations, and Islamic youth centres across the country to root out extremism.

Cohesion and coherence

As we have seen, then, how far texts are made cohesive depends on the judgement of the producers of the texts (in speech or writing) about what meanings they can assume the text receivers can work out for themselves by invoking what the they know about the world. Cohesive devices are only aids to understanding and can only be effective to the extent that they enable readers (or listeners) to construct meaning that makes contextual sense to them, in other words to the extent that the cohesion in the text enables them to derive a **coherent** discourse from it. It follows from this that it is possible for a text to be cohesive but incoherent. For example:

> The process may seem complicated but actually it is not really, so long as you prepare things in advance and know what has to be done in what order. Some of the things you need you may already have, but others, of course, you may need to get. They are not always readily available and when they are they can be quite expensive. But the final result will make all the effort and cost worthwhile.

Here we have a text that is co-textually well connected with cohesive devices: *it* relates anaphorically to *the process*, *others* and *they* to *things*, *cost* links semantically to *expensive*, and so on. The trouble is that the reader cannot key the text into a context so as to make sense of it (*process*—what process? *things*—what things?). We cannot tell what this text is supposed to be about because we have no schematic frame of reference to refer these terms to. We could provide one, by giving the text a title: for example *Cooking Chicken Biryani*. Once a frame of reference is provided, the contextual connection can be made, and the meaning then falls coherently into place.

How far you can make coherent sense of a text depends, then, on how far you can relate it to a frame of reference. This is obviously true of this rather curious example (specially invented to make the point). But it is also true of any other text. Take the one we were looking at earlier about the Muslim Council. Here too an external frame of reference is presupposed. Consider the phrase *the terrorist threat*. The definite article signals shared knowledge, but there has been no mention of such a threat in the text itself. It is assumed that readers will already know about it and will relate what is said in the text to the situation in Britain at the time, the bombings in London in the summer of 2005, the danger of Islamic extremists and so on.

A frame of reference is what was referred to in the preceding chapter as an ideational schema. A passage can also be cohesive as text but lack coherence as discourse because it does not key the reader into any familiar schema of an interpersonal kind. Consider the following:

We spent our holidays in Romania. This is a country where grapes are grown. They are a kind of fruit. So are bananas. Fruit contains vitamins, and these are essential for a healthy life. So is regular exercise. Jogging is good for you. We do it every day ...

There is no shortage here of cohesive links across the different parts of the text. *They* is a pro-form that links to *grapes*, *so* is a pro-form that serves as an anaphoric token of both *a kind of fruit* and *essential for a healthy life*, *jogging* makes a semantic connection with the preceding *exercise*, and so on. But cohesive though it is, it is a very odd kind of text, and it is difficult to make any coherent sense of it. Unlike the previous passage, it is not that we cannot key the text into a familiar frame of reference, but rather that the frame of reference keeps shifting: first it seems that the passage is to be about holidays in Romania, and then the topic shifts to grapes, and then fruit in general, and then vitamins and then ... The problem here is not so much that we cannot understand what is being said but that we cannot see the point of saying it. In other words, we do not recognize its purpose because it does not correspond with the communicative conventions of any genre we are familiar with. And so we find it incoherent as discourse, cohesive though it is as text.

Conclusion

The general point to be made is that no matter how cohesive a text may be in terms of internal co-textual links that can be identified, the extent to which it is interpreted as coherent discourse will always depend on how far it can be related externally to contextual realities, to the ideational and interpersonal schemata that readers are familiar with in the particular socio-cultural world they live in.

6
The negotiation of meaning

Systemic and schematic knowledge

As we have seen in the last two chapters, the process of communication involves the engagement of two kinds of knowledge.
In Chapter 4 we saw how people make sense of text, whether
spoken or written, by relating it to what they know of the world
they live in, the ideational and interpersonal schemata that
represent the customary and conventional ways in which their
socio-cultural reality is structured. This we can refer to as
schematic knowledge. But people also need a knowledge of what
is semantically encoded in the language itself in order for this
schematic knowledge to be pragmatically activated as appropriate. Thus, as we saw in Chapter 5, a reader of a text has to know
that particular pro-forms have a semantic relationship with other
expressions in a text in order to recognize them as cohesively
linked. To realize what the word *she* refers to pragmatically
(by intention or interpretation) it is necessary to know that it
encodes the semantic features of singular animate and female.
This is not sufficient to identify the relevant reference, but it is
necessary. We can call this knowledge of what is encoded in the
language system itself **systemic knowledge**.

It is important to note, however, that neither kind of knowledge is fixed. They provide us with a necessary starting point
in making meaning, but as communication proceeds they are
subject to modification. Certain textual features, for example,
may serve to key the reader or listener in to a particular schema
but as the discourse develops this may be extended, altered, or even
abandoned altogether. So schematic knowledge provides us with
a set of default assumptions: it projects provisional expectations

which are subject to on-line revision as we proceed in deriving discourse from text. Although, as we have seen in Chapter 4, the schemata that we are familiar with will dispose us to interpret a text along certain lines, they do not therefore *determine* our interpretation. If they did, not only would we never learn anything new, but we could hardly be said to be engaging in communication at all.

Communicative convergence

For communication is always a matter of negotiating some kind of common agreement between the parties in an interaction. The first-person party, the sender (**P1**), formulates a message by drawing on systemic and schematic knowledge and the second-person party, the receiver (**P2**), brings similar knowledge to bear in interpretation. Communication is effective to the extent that there is some convergence between the two. We might represent this by the following diagram:

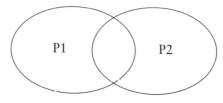

How much convergence is achieved in the communication will naturally depend on there being a measure of correspondence between P1 and P2 knowledge. Thus problems might arise if P1 uses items of language outside P2's competence, or refers to an ideational framework that P2 does not know about, or follows interpersonal conventions that P2 is unfamiliar with. Where the communication is enacted through the immediately reciprocal interaction of conversation, such problems can be resolved by negotiating meaning 'on-line': P2 can ask for clarification, or elicit additional information, or let the problem pass in the hope that it will get sorted out as the conversation develops, seeking perhaps to steer the interaction towards that end. P1, if sensitive to the problem, may try to resolve it by subsequently elaborating on the message, or reformulating it in different terms. As was pointed out in Chapter 1, when there is no joint production of text, as in written language use, and so no possibility of such reciprocal on-line adjustment, P1 has to somehow anticipate what problems the intended P2 might have. Conversely, P2, free of the need to take part in the co-construction of conversation, is under no constraint to make any particular adjustment, or indeed to make any adjustment at all. All of which explains, in part at least, why writing is a relatively difficult ability to acquire, and reading a relatively easy one.

Communication on this account, then, is a matter of the parties concerned negotiating a measure of convergence. Some degree of correspondence in the prior knowledge of P1 and P2 has to exist beforehand, of course, for otherwise there is nothing to negotiate with in the first place, and the closer the correspondence, clearly, the easier it is, potentially, to converge, and the less close the greater the need to negotiate a convergence. But it is important to note that the degree to which the parties actually converge does not just depend on how far they are able to do so; it also depends, crucially, on how far they want or need to do so. In other words, the degree of convergence that we seek to achieve is regulated by the purpose of our communication. Convergence is always only partial. Although we may say that we understand somebody perfectly well, what we mean is that we understand them well *enough*. Mutual understanding is never, and never can be, perfect but only approximate to purpose. So even though texts may have the appearance of being fixed and complete, the discourse we derive from them is always indeterminate and partial. No matter how cohesive a text may be, whatever coherent sense we make of it is negotiable.

Negotiating convergence

For communication to take place, then, for texts to realize a discourse function, the two parties involved, P1 and P2, have also to be parties to an agreement to co-operate in negotiating a convergence, a meeting of minds, a mutual understanding, whereby meaning is achieved as required by their purpose in communicating. So it is that what P1 intends to mean and what P2 interprets P1 as meaning come into correspondence. How close this correspondence actually is on a particular occasion is not easy to tell. The two parties may, after all, be at cross-purposes. But even if they are not, P1 may intend more, or less, than P2 takes in. P2 may, knowingly or not, only partially understand what P1 is talking about. And we need to bear in mind as well that, as was discussed in Chapter 2, there are different kinds of pragmatic meaning that are to be negotiated in communication, and the two parties may negotiate one successfully but not another. So P2 may understand what P1 intends to refer to by saying something, but not what illocutionary force is intended, or may recognize the intended force but not grasp what effect it is meant to have.

Bringing our knowledge (both systemic and schematic) to bear in an appropriate way so as to converge on agreed meaning is, then, a complex process, and it is a process that we only embark upon in the first place if we are prepared to co-operate. But then we also need to know what the accepted procedures or ground rules are for the co-operative negotiation of meaning.

The co-operative principle

The philosopher Paul Grice has proposed that when people converse they tacitly subscribe to what he calls the **co-operative principle**. Although he has conversation in mind, one can, as we shall see later, apply the same principle to all kinds of communication, whether this takes the form of conversation or not. Grice suggests that the co-operative principle can be expressed in terms of four **maxims** that parties in an interaction will subscribe to, on condition that both of them also recognize the purpose for which they are communicating in the first place. This is an important proviso, which we will return to later.

The quantity maxim

One of these maxims or negotiating rules is what Grice refers to as the *quantity maxim*: do not provide more, or less, information than is necessary. This relates to the least effort principle in communication that was discussed in Chapter 5, where it was pointed out that how much actual text is produced is regulated by assumptions about shared contextual knowledge, including a knowledge of schematic conventions. Clearly there is no need to provide information by means of language if it is already common knowledge. Of course, the assumptions that first-person parties make about this can be wrong. If they underestimate how much context is shared and so over-textualize by producing too much language, then what they say will be heard or read as pointlessly wordy, or verbose. If, on the other hand, they overestimate the extent of shared contextual knowledge, and so under-textualize, then what they say will be heard or read as obscure. Notice again that contextual knowledge includes a knowledge of schematic conventions. So some genres will require a quantity of language which would be quite inappropriate in another. Texts which are designed to meet legal requirements, for example, like contracts, insurance policies, or the small print on the back of an airline ticket, will textualize meanings in great detail because it serves the purpose of this genre to do so. But the same degree of textualization would be absurdly excessive elsewhere.

Or take the case of public notices that were discussed in the first chapter of this book. When taking a stroll through a park in London, for example, you are likely to come across notices of two kinds. One (usually near the entrance) is a text in relatively small print which is an official display of the by-laws regulating the use of the park. It specifies in considerable detail what is legally allowed and prohibited there, often ending with the phrase: BY ORDER, and the name, perhaps even the signature, of some person in authority. We might well also come across a quite different kind of notice, like KEEP OFF THE GRASS: a very short text in relatively large print. We would be surprised to find such a notice couched in the official legal language of a by-law. The point is that both uses of language conform to the conventions of their genre, and are appropriate to their different purposes. Both are in accordance with the maxim of quantity.

One thing to note about this maxim, then, is that, if it is to serve its co-operative function, its application must depend on context and purpose. A second thing to note is that people may choose not to apply it anyway. As has already been mentioned, a PI (a first-person party) may intend to be co-operative but make a wrong calculation about common knowledge and so fail to conform to the maxim by mistake. When this occurs in conversation, it is generally possible to repair the situation on-line. But the first-person party may not intend to be co-operative and may deliberately flout the maxim by saying more or less than the occasion requires. What then? What happens then is that, if the flouting is recognized, P1 (the speaker, or writer) is taken to be expressing some significance over and above what the language would appear to indicate. The result is what Grice calls a **conversational implicature**.

Conversational implicature

Imagine, for example, that you are called as a witness in a court of law, and, having sworn to tell the truth, the whole truth, and nothing but the truth, you are asked the following question by the counsel for the prosecution:

> Could you tell the court what you did on the morning of February 10th.

And you reply:

> I was woken by the alarm clock at 7.15 in the morning. I got out of bed. I put on my slippers and went to the bedroom door and opened it. I then walked to the bathroom and turned on the cold tap over the washbasin, took my toothbrush and cleaned my teeth ...

It is unlikely you would get much further, or even as far as this. It will be made plain to you that in effect you are in violation of the quantity maxim in that you are providing the court with more information than is required for its purposes. You may claim that you are trying to tell the whole truth, but if the judge suspects that you know perfectly well that by convention this means only that part of the truth that cannot be inferred from common knowledge, he, or she, will assume you are being deliberately perverse and that your real intention is not to co-operate as a witness should, but to mock the proceedings. You will have created an implicature and if you continue you are likely to be penalized for contempt of court.

Implicatures can also be created by saying less, not more, than convention requires. Take the case of a certain (fictional)

Professor Parsons Green who has been asked to provide a reference in support of a student (a certain fictional Ms Justine Case) who is applying for a research grant. Professor Parsons Green is, of course, familiar with the genre, and assumes that the recipient of the reference will be too. His letter reads as follows:

Dear Professor Chiswick,

Justine Case
Ms Case was a student of mine last year. She completed her course and always returned her books promptly to the library. Yours sincerely,

Hugo Parsons Green.
Professor of Plant Propagation
University of Kew

Professor Green knows full well that the genre of a letter of reference requires much more content than this. He knows that what is expected is information about the course of study referred to and what grades Ms Case got, together with an evaluation of her ability, scholarly aptitude, and so on. He is clearly deliberately flouting the maxim of quantity here and creating an implicature, in effect signalling that he has an entirely negative opinion of Ms Case, but without saying so explicitly. Since Professor Chiswick will also be familiar with the conventions of the genre, he will be in doubt that this letter is—in no uncertain terms (all the more certain, indeed, because the terms are so few)—a letter of *non*-recommendation.

These are, of course, extreme examples of maxim violation and the implicatures it gives rise too. Furthermore, they are fictional. In real life, our frequent disregard of the maxim is generally less blatant, and the implicatures more subtle. When people say more than seems warranted, we might suspect them of 'beating about the bush' so as to impress us, or hide something from us under their verbiage. When people are sparing with their commendation, we suspect them of 'damning with faint praise'. Regulating how much language we use to conform to the quantity maxim, and exploiting the maxim to create implicatures to add further significance to what we say, are complex and elusive processes. We shall have more to say about them in the next chapter.

The maxims of quality, relation, and manner

Meanwhile, there are still three other maxims to talk about in this chapter. One of them is what Grice calls the *quality maxim*: be truthful and do not say things you know to be false. So, for example, if I tell you that it is raining outside, you will assume that I have good grounds for saying so, that I am not just saying it for fun, or to deceive you. But this maxim too is frequently violated. So even if it is raining outside, I might come out with an obvious falsehood like: 'Lovely weather today,' and if we both know full well that the weather is appalling, this results in an implicature. You recognize that I am flouting the quality maxim in order to lend an extra significance to what I say, to create, in this case, the effect of irony.

Irony is not the only effect that is brought about by the deliberate denial of this maxim. It can lend extra emphasis to what is said, as in the following:

This bag weighs a ton.
The drinks cost a fortune.
My brother is a pig.
I'm starving.

And so on.

People who say things like this do not intend them to be taken literally (the bag does not really weigh a ton, and my brother is not really a pig) though sometimes in striving for even more emphasis they might actually say 'This bag *literally* weighs a ton', 'I'm *literally* starving', thereby flouting the maxim of quality twice over.

The deliberate non-compliance with the maxim of quality is a very common feature of communication. Indeed the maxim is probably as much honoured in the breach as in the observance, and the breaching gives rise to the creativity of ordinary language in the use of metaphor and other figurative turns of phrase. Thus we read in the newspaper about politicians being poodles and puppets, about their painting over the cracks, splitting hairs, stabbing each other in the back, about their ideas being floated, shot down, torn to shreds, put on the back burner, and so on. And these are only examples that have become established expressions. The deliberate flouting of this maxim is a naturally creative process that goes on all the time.

As with the quantity maxim, we should again note that compliance with this quality maxim is regulated by what is conventionally appropriate. There are genres which sanction the expression of falsehood, or at least being economical with the truth. In an obituary, for example, or funeral oration, it is expected that you will exaggerate the virtues and avoid mentioning anything unpalatable about the deceased. Here compliance with the maxim would require you *not* to tell the whole truth and nothing but the truth, but on the contrary, more like everything *but* the truth.

A third maxim is that of *relation*: make what you say relevant to the topic or purpose of the communication. One way of illustrating compliance with this maxim is by reference to how adjacency pairs work in turn taking, as discussed earlier in Chapter 4. Thus a question sets the conditions of relevance for the answer that follows. Imagine a little domestic scene: a husband and wife getting ready to go out for an evening. The wife asks the husband:

Wife: How do you like my new hat?

If the husband is inclined to be co-operative, comply with the relation maxim and make his turn relevant, then he would recognize that the purpose of the question is to elicit an answer, and that the answer should make reference to the hat, for that is the topic his wife has introduced into the conversation. The following then would all count as relevant (and cohesive) replies:

Husband: Very much.
Husband: Looks nice.
Husband: Well, not sure it is quite your colour.

And so on.

But, of course, the husband (for some reason or another) may not be in co-operative mood and may choose not to comply with the maxim.

Husband: It's ten past eight already.

This remark is irrelevant on two counts: it does not function as an answer to the question and it makes no reference to the topic of the hat. In consequence, there is an implicature: the husband's utterance has a significance over and above its apparent meaning. Without access to more contextual information, it is, of course, impossible to say what exactly its significance might be. Perhaps he is avoiding a negative response (*I hate the hat*) or expressing his indifference (*Who cares about hats*) or his impatience (*This is no time to bother about hats, we're late*). There is no way of knowing.

Compliance with this maxim is again, as with the others, regulated by convention. To return for a moment to Professor Parsons Green and his letter of reference. Even if he had met genre requirements by keeping to the maxims of quantity and quality and provided full and truthful information about Ms Justine Case, if it was all about such things as her personal appearance and her punctual attendance at lectures with no reference at all to her scholarly abilities or achievements, it would not have been relevant to the purpose, and so it would still have created a similar implicature of disapproval.

The fourth of the Gricean maxims is that of *manner*: be clear, avoid ambiguity and obscurity. This maxim has to do with what Hymes refers to as feasibility, which was discussed in Chapter 2. Unintentional violations of this maxim can have comical consequences, as in the following examples of ambiguous newspaper headlines:

DRUNK GETS NINE MONTHS IN VIOLIN CASE
RED TAPE HOLDS UP NEW BRIDGE

By convention, the quantity maxim is appropriately applied in newspaper headlines to concentrate as much information into as few words as possible. This can result in expressions which are, in the Hymes sense, not normally *grammatically* possible (noun phrases without determiners, for example) or not normally appropriate (simple present tense used to refer to past events as in *gets, holds* in these headlines). As we can see from the ambiguity in these examples, keeping appropriately to the quantity maxim can result in the unintentional violation of the manner maxim.

But not all violations are unintentional, of course. They can also be exploited to produce deliberate ambiguity so as to attract attention. With headlines, it is not always easy to tell whether the ambiguity is intended or not. In the examples given above, it seems clear it is not. In *Time* magazine of 20 February 2006, however, there is an article about Olympic athletes adding or switching passports to achieve their ambitions. It bears the title:

WAIVING THE FLAG

Here we can be sure that the manner maxim is knowingly flouted to create an ambiguous effect, as is the case with the following advertising slogans:

> If you want to get ahead get a hat
> The car in front is a Toyota
> Nokia—connecting people

We said earlier that for communication to take place, the parties involved have to co-operate in negotiating some degree of agreed convergence, and that these maxims can be taken as a set of ground rules for doing so. And yet, as we have seen, people do not always keep to the rules. Why then do they not always co-operate? Why do they so often say more, or less, than they need to? Why are they not always truthful, relevant, and straightforward in what they say? If people are so often uncooperative on purpose, what is the purpose?

In communication two parties co-operate to converge on common ground. For this to happen there has to be some give and take on both sides: each party has to concede some ground of their own. This ground represents his/her own individual reality, a sense of self, a personal territory of identity, which it is their natural instinct to assert and protect. Co-operation necessarily involves some encroachment on this individual life space, and the area of convergence is always a potential site of contention between self and other. There has to be give and take, but on whose terms? Who gives way, and who takes advantage? How far is the common ground actually an invasion of your own personal space?

Co-operative and territorial imperatives

So, on the one hand, for communication to take place at all, you have to co-operate, but, on the other, there is always the risk that this will compromise your own individuality. So this **co-operative imperative** is countered by another that acts against it—a **territorial imperative**, a need to preserve and protect one's own space— just as powerfully instinctive in humans as in other creatures, and there is continual tension between them which has to be somehow reconciled. So it is not just meaning that is negotiated in communication but human relations. P1 and P2 are not just parties seeking an impartial agreement about shared knowledge but individual personalities competing to establish their own **position** in the area of convergence.

These uncooperative floutings of the maxims we have been considering can be understood as assertions of self, signs of the territorial imperative at work. As we have seen, the implicatures that result from them can give extra emphasis to what is said, or an undertone of irony or contempt. They project a personal attitude or point of view: 'This is my position, this is where I stand on this matter.' So one reason for disregarding the maxims is to assert territorial rights, so to speak, and to project one's self. But there is another reason. Co-operation involves encroachment, and this will often need to be tactfully managed. An incursion into the other's space may not be welcome. It may involve an adjustment the other is not prepared to make, or a threat to **face** or self-esteem, and this may cause offence, or embarrassment, a 'loss of face'. The other may react in ways that threaten your own face. It is generally in our interests to maintain good relations by a mutual respect for face and the territorial rights of the other. This kind of co-operation which, paradoxically enough, calls for the non-cooperative departure from the maxims, goes under the general name of politeness. So there will be occasions when we avoid telling the truth because we want to reinforce the other's self-esteem, not undermine it, when we are deliberately uninformative or irrelevant because giving a direct answer might cause offence, and we prefer to leave it to the other to take responsibility for inferring the appropriate implicature.

Conclusion

Although the violation of the maxims of the kind we have been considering have to do with small-scale adjustments that are made in conversational negotiation, they are symptomatic of how the co-operative and territorial imperatives operate in discourse as a whole, written as well as spoken, for the assertion of self and the manipulation of the other, and generally of how language is used for persuasion and the control of opinion. These are matters that are taken up in the next chapter.

7
Critical analysis

Positioning

As we have seen in the last chapter, communication is not only a matter of the parties concerned finding a form of words which will serve most efficiently to indicate what reference and force they intend. It also involves finding words that will have the desired effect—that is to say, words which are tactically effective in regulating the **position** of self in relation to the other. For all communication, to a greater or lesser extent, is an exercise in control, an attempt to assert one's own position and to persuade the other to accept it. When somebody says, or writes, something it is with the intention of getting the addressee, the second-person party to think or feel or act in a certain way, and the maxim violations we considered in the last chapter can be seen as tactics that are used for the purpose.

Such tactics are not, however, confined to negotiations in the face-to-face interaction of conversation. They find expression in a number of ways in all language use, and it is the purpose of this chapter to see whether we can track some of them down. We can begin by returning to the text that was first discussed in Chapter 2:

> At the height of the Kosovo crisis in May 1999, Tony Blair was on his way to Bucharest, the Romanian capital, to drum up local support for Nato's high-risk confrontation with Serbia. The Prime Minister astonished his advisers by suddenly announcing on the aeroplane that he was going to promise Romania early membership of the European Union in return for its continued backing.

Terms of reference

The point was made in our earlier discussion that, if you have the required schematic knowledge, you will understand the expression *The prime minister* as an alternative term for *Tony Blair*. The quite different wordings have the same referent. But then, we might ask, why not just use one of them? Why the variation, and what motivates the choice of one wording rather than another? One explanation might be that the writer wants to keep to the quantity maxim by avoiding redundancy and not saying the same thing twice, thereby avoiding a possible implicature: the reader might infer some significance in the repetition. But then, why not use the pronoun *he* to make a normal anaphoric link? The expression *The Prime Minister* refers not to the person but to the position of Tony Blair and one might suggest that in using it, the writer is giving deferential recognition to his official status. The simple anaphoric pronoun would, of course, have no such significance, and nor would another alternative *Mr Blair*, which, though suggesting respect, still relates to person. And had the writer used the expression *Tony* here, this would have been suggestive of a kind of personal familiarity with no sign of respect at all.

We can locate these different **terms of reference** on a scale of increasing deference or respect.

Tony—Tony Blair—Mr Blair—The Prime Minister

But this does not exhaust the number of terms that might be used in reference to Tony Blair. Even less respectful terms might be *our Tony* or an expression like *Bush's Poodle*, which plainly flouts the quality maxim. Seemingly more respectful expressions would be *The present incumbent of 10 Downing Street*, *The head of Her Majesty's government*. However, they may be only *seemingly* more respectful—for if they were to be used in this particular text, these expressions could be taken as flouting the maxim of quantity (they give more information than is needed here) or the maxim of manner (they are over-elaborate) and in this case they would give rise to implicatures that indicate irony and the very opposite of respect.

The general question that arises from this discussion is what motivates the use of one expression rather than another. And we are not only talking about the kinds of terms of reference we have just been examining in this particular text. Every use of language involves selection and so every text can be rewritten in other terms—terms that could have been chosen, but, for one reason or another, were not. For one reason or another. What, then, might these reasons be?

Alternative wordings and persuasive purpose

Let us first note that, as pointed out in the discussion of thematization in Chapter 5, a language will always provide the resource for alternative wordings: there will always be different grammatical structures and different lexical items available for referring to the 'same' thing in a variety of ways, thereby allowing for the expression of attitude, personal evaluation, point of view. In some cases, such expression is allowed for by different **connotations** that are assigned to lexical items by convention. Thus we can find in English terms that correspond in denotation, but are marked for negative or positive evaluation. For example, adjectives like *idealistic, single-minded, self-assured* are generally taken as positive, whereas the corresponding words *doctrinaire, narrow-minded, cocky* are generally taken as negative. The verbs *withdraw, decline,* and *negotiate* are usually positive, *retreat, refuse,* and *haggle* negative. The nouns *gathering* and *colleague* are usually positive, *mob* and *crony* negative. And so on. It might be supposed, then, that if you want to indicate attitude, the lexical means are available to you to do so. So if you were to tell me about a doctrinaire, narrow-minded, cocky politician and his mob of cronies, I will be in little doubt about what view you take of this person (who I, as one of his colleagues, may have always considered idealistic, single-minded, and self-assured).

But things are not so straightforward. To begin with, the vocabulary of English is not all conveniently marked for attitude in this way. And anyway, words are not put to use in isolation but are incorporated into lexical and grammatical patterns in texts where, as we have seen, they are acted upon by other words in complex and unpredictable ways. And the texts themselves contract complex and unpredictable relations with context. So what words mean by convention (as recorded in a dictionary) and what people mean by them on a particular occasion of use are two quite different things. People do not keep to the Gricean maxims, and they do not keep to semantic convention either. What they mean is not always apparent from what they say. This being so, we obviously cannot infer an underlying attitude or point of view directly from the wording in a text.

And yet there must surely be something in texts that provides evidence of such attitude. There is no doubt that every text, spoken or written, is composed of variants which could be replaced by alternative wordings. For every text that is composed there are other texts that could have been composed but were not. We have argued too that texts are composed to realize a discourse by bringing about a schematic convergence of minds. The convergence, as we have seen in the last chapter, is subject to continual and contested negotiation with both parties seeking to control the common ground—in other words, seeking to get their message across, to get their own discourse accepted. So a particular textual choice must surely be motivated by this persuasive purpose.

Critical discourse analysis

It is just such a conviction that informs work that has been done in the name of **critical discourse analysis (CDA)**. Those who follow this approach are particularly concerned with (and concerned about) the use (and abuse) of language for the exercise of socio-political power. In the first chapter of this book, it was noted that what somebody might mean by producing a text could be related to broader issues of ideology and social belief, and it is these issues that CDA is concerned with. What its proponents are interested in is **discourse** in a rather different sense from that we have been discussing in this book: for them, discourses are kinds of genre, institutionalized modes of thinking and social practice, and those who compose texts are taken to be not so much individuals as socially constructed spokespersons or representatives of discourse communities. So critical discourse analysts enquire into the role played by schematic knowledge, as we have done in earlier chapters of this book, but the schemata they focus on have to do more with socio-political values and beliefs, not only with ideational but also ideological representations of reality, not only with cultural constructs of how the world is, but also with political constructs of how it should be. And in their view people are not only influenced by ideology but they actually construct it in what they say, and in ways that are most likely to persuade others to comply with it.

The task that CDA sets itself is to discover traces of ideological bias in texts. They undertake this not just as an academic exercise in analysis but as a campaign against what is seen to be a stealthy undercover operation by those in power to control opinion to their own advantage. CDA is critical in the sense that it calls into question ideas and assumptions that have become taken for granted as self-evidently valid on the grounds that they actually preserve a status quo which in effect sustains inequality and injustice by privileging the elite and the powerful at the expense of everybody else. So CDA is committed to a cause and puts its own ideological agenda up front. Its proponents are not simply analysts but activists. The question arises, however, as to how far these two roles can be reconciled.

Identifying the significance of textual choice

CDA, then, adopts the position that particular textual choices are motivated and focus attention on those which are ideologically motivated, and more particularly when the ideology acts against the interests of the deprived and the oppressed. Now one might raise the question at this point about what it means to say that the choice of a particular expression is motivated. Does it mean that the choice is deliberate? How do we know that unless we consult the person who composed the text? This we usually cannot do, and even if we could, we might not get a straight answer. Perhaps the writer is not aware of making any choice at all, but is simply using different expressions in free variation. In this case, surely, nothing of any significance attaches to the use of one rather than another. Not necessarily, though, one might argue: for the choice of a particular expression may well be made subliminally, below the level of conscious awareness, and so can still be taken as evidence of an underlying ideological attitude, all the more insidious, indeed, for being instinctive. Writers, and speakers, might be unaware of the underlying ideological significance that lurks in the textual variants they produce. Similarly, readers, and listeners, may be unaware of the indoctrinating effects these variants have upon them. This, the argument runs, is why we need critical analysis: to reveal to the unwary language user the ideological influences they may be unwittingly subscribing to.

Implicatures and lexical choice

How then might such a critical analysis be conducted? We can begin by considering again the possible implicatures that arise from maxim violations. To take a simple lexical example. Suppose that in reading a newspaper article about immigration, I come across the expression *an army of refugees*. Here, as indeed with any metaphor, we have a clear denial of the quality maxim. It is not true that these refugees are an army, so why has the writer chosen this expression rather than, for example, *a large number of refugees* or *a crowd of refugees*, both of which would adequately indicate that there are a lot of them? One answer might be that in choosing the word *army*, the writer indicates not only that these refugees are numerous, but that they are dangerous, thereby signalling a negative attitude to them. What about other features embedded in the word? An army is dangerous because it is armed, organized, disciplined, controlled by some central command. Is there an implication here that the refugees resemble an army in these respects as well? Perhaps not. But then how do we know? A metaphor recategorizes something as something else, but only in certain respects. But in which respects in this case? Refugees are categorized as an army. But which features of the word *army* are activated when it is used here in reference to refugees? Just the general feature of it being dangerous, we might say, and not other features. But why not the other features? And why is the feature of being dangerous activated in this case? It is easy enough to find other expressions where this feature is not activated at all. Thus a sampling of the British National Corpus of English will reveal armies of earwigs, weeds, chickens, fans, helpers, supporters, shoppers, and little boys.

Implicatures and grammatical choice

Clearly there are difficulties in inferring significance by focusing on particular lexical items. We might then turn our attention to grammar. Here too, as we saw in Chapter 5 in the discussion of thematization and information structure, the language provides abundant resources for composing alternative expressions, and therefore, one might suggest (if critically inclined) of indicating attitude, of giving what is said a particular bias. Let us suppose that in our newspaper text on immigration we read the following:

> The refugees were driven back and many of them were injured.

Here we have a passive structure with a deleted agent (*were injured (by ?)*). What then, we might ask, motivates the deletion? The use of this construction can be said to go against the quantity maxim in that information has been withheld. Who did the driving back and injuring? The police perhaps? We are not told. Is there then some attempt here to gloss over the responsibility? If the alternative, full, form of the passive had been used, there would have to be some specification of agent:

> The refugees were driven back by the police and many of them were injured by the police.

With the passive, the grammar does not constrain you to provide an agent. The active alternative, of course does:

> The police drove back the refugees and injured many of them.

But there is, as we noted in Chapter 5, another feature of the active alternative. The agent as grammatical subject becomes thematized, and so now, we might suggest, agency (and so responsibility) is foregrounded as the topic, so if you wanted to play down the active role of the police, you would presumably want to avoid using this construction.

There are then three grammatical alternatives here and we might propose that which is used depends on the writer's take on this event. If the intention is to represent it as something that just happens to the refugees, then the structure to go for would be the passive with agent deleted and the refugees as theme. This choice would then indicate an attitude favourable to the police. In the case where, for one reason or another, the writer felt reluctantly obliged to mention the police at all, reference could be tucked away in a prepositional phrase in the rheme. But if, on the other hand, the writer wanted to focus on what the police did to the refugees, then the preferred structure would be the active variant with the police thematized, thereby reflecting an unfavourable attitude to them.

But, again, things are not that straightforward, for the simple reason that these inferences of significance are, again, drawn from language items in isolation—in this case structures rather than words—without regard to the co-textual relations they contract with other parts of the text. Only when we look at textual continuity can we decide on whether or not the writer is conforming to the quantity maxim. Let us, for example, suppose that there is some text that comes before the structure we started with:

> Hundreds of protesting refugees then began to move in the direction of the parliament buildings, where the police confronted them. The refugees/They were driven back and many of them were injured.

One cannot reasonably argue that to use the agentless passive here would be to withhold information about agency, for this information is already given, explicitly provided in the preceding sentence. As was indicated in our discussion of cohesion earlier, how a particular part of a text is understood depends on its connection with what has gone before. So it is that we understand the pronoun *them* in the second sentence of this text as referring anaphorically to the refugees (and not to the parliament buildings). There is no need to spell this out. And similarly there is no need to spell out the agency role of the police in the last sentence. Indeed, to do so would run the risk of violating the quantity maxim by giving *too much* information. As was pointed out in Chapter 5, the cohesive devices we considered there follow a least effort principle. As such they serve an essentially co-operative purpose, for their function is to regulate information in relation to what is already given or known to make it easier to process.

There is a related point to be noted about the phrase *The refugees* in the second sentence. Occurring as the first constituent, this is theme, and there is something odd about it. Now as was pointed out in Chapter 5 a theme can either serve as topic (what P1 is talking about) or given (what P2 already knows). The refugees have already been referred to in the noun phrase that appears as theme in the first sentence (*Hundreds of protesting refugees*), and here it seems reasonable to interpret it as topic (since there is no preceding text to refer to). But since this topic has already been established, this would surely incline us to interpret the occurrence of *The refugees* as theme in the second sentence as given. That being so, it would seem normal to minimize the reference and use a pro-form, and indeed, on the evidence of the reaction of a number of informants, the text would be more natural if the second sentence were to read *They were driven back* ...

This is not to say that a particular thematization or the selection of the agentless passive, or any other structure for that matter may not be ideologically significant, or be indicative of a particular position that P1 wants to impose on P2. But the point is that we cannot tell from the simple fact of its occurrence in a text. The structure alone does not signal its own significance.

Conclusion

Clearly language is widely used, and abused, as a means of control and persuasion, and it is one of the main purposes of discourse study (perhaps indeed the primary purpose) to develop a well-grounded understanding of how this is done. But just as clearly, it makes little sense to assign ideological significance to the occurrence of lexical and grammatical features as such without regard to the co-textual relations they contract with other features. Some of these were discussed in Chapter 5 when we looked at cohesion. Developments in corpus linguistics over recent years have revealed other kinds of co-textual connection. What these are, and how far they contribute to a better informed and more critical understanding of discourse are matters taken up in the next (and last) chapter of this book.

8
Text analysis

Actually attested language

Here we take up again matters that have been mentioned earlier in the book. In Chapter 1, the point was made that communication involves the production of text to indicate intended meaning. In Chapter 2, reference was made to Hymes' account of communicative competence, in which he suggests that when confronted with a text in a particular language we, as competent users of that language, are capable of making four kinds of judgement about it. We can say how far it is possible, that is to say how far it conforms to what is lexically and grammatically encoded in the language. In this case, we treat the text simply as a collection of linguistic elements. But texts are normally only produced if there is an intention to communicate a message of some kind and the other three kinds of judgement have to do with this normal communicative functioning of text. Thus we can say how far a particular text is feasible, that is to say, how easy it is to process, and this, as we have seen, will depend on how it keys in with shared knowledge. How far it is appropriate (the third kind of judgement) will also, crucially, depend on how the text can be related to context to bring about reference, force, and effect.

The fourth kind of judgement has to do with whether and to what extent a particular text is attested as actually occurring usage. Here we are concerned with conformity not to linguistic rule but conventions of usage. As has already been pointed out, communication involves the selective use of the encoded resources of lexis and grammar, and we have been looking at what motivation there might be for the selection of one possibility rather than another. We have already looked at ways in which the feasibility and appropriateness factors may affect selection. But we also need to consider which selections are generally preferred by convention. Though all lexical and grammatical elements are equally possible in the linguistic code, they are obviously not all equally common in actual usage. How then does this fourth factor of the actually performed relate to the other factors in the process of communication?

Norms of usage

With the advent of the computer, we are now in a position to provide exact descriptions of actual usage. Vast quantities of text can be collected into a **corpus** and electronically analysed. As a result, it is now possible to establish the relative frequency of occurrence of words and structures either in particular domains of use or more generally across domains to provide profiles of frequency in the language as a whole. We therefore have a norm of usage against which we can establish the relative (ab)normality of the occurrence of a word or structure in a particular text. If it is abnormally rare, we might then infer that its selection goes against the manner maxim and so creates an implicature. So, to take a simple example, if somebody in a conversation were to talk about *circumventing a hindrance* rather than *getting round a problem*, you would suppose that they were trying to impress or striving for a comic effect. An extreme example of abnormal usage is to be found in Henry Green's novel *Living*, with its very infrequent use of one of the most frequently occurring words in the English language, the definite article *the*:

> They had taken bus. They had gone Saturday afternoon to Mr Jones' uncle and aunt that were lodge-keepers at gate of big house one mile out from bus terminus.

This avoidance of the definite article results in impossible sentences (in the Hymes sense) and, together with other deliberate abnormalities, is intended by the author, on his own testimony, to represent the basic simplicities of everyday working life.

Corpus analysis can tell us not only about the overall frequency of words, but also about their **range**, that is to say their distribution in different domains of use. The words *circumvent* and *hindrance*, for example, uncommon though they are, might well be found quite often in certain kinds of legal genre. They would then constitute a local norm of appropriate usage. The same point can be made even about the definite article. Though this word is generally recorded as having a higher frequency and wider range than almost any other in the English language, it is quite normal for it to be omitted in newspaper headlines.

So relative frequency can be taken as having a schematic significance in that certain words mark particular genres or discourse domains. Thus the words *customer, consumer, product, marketing, retailer, sales* will be shown to have a much higher concentration in business domains than in any other genre. And again, if they were to show up in comparable numbers elsewhere this would be noticed as abnormal and the question would naturally arise as to what the motivation for such non-conformity might be. If these terms occurred in the discourse domain of clinical medicine or education, for example, one might infer that the writer's attitude to health care or education is that it is just a kind of commodity to be produced and retailed in response to market forces like any other.

Patterns of collocation

It is not, however, only the simple frequency and range of single items that is revealed in the corpus analysis of text but also, more interestingly and significantly, the frequency and range of their patterns of co-occurrence with other items. In Chapter 5 we looked at the kind of co-textual links that are established on-line to establish cohesion whereby the pro-form *he*, for example, makes an anaphoric connection with the preceding noun phrase *The Prime Minister*. But there are also other connections across linguistic items, certain patterns of co-occurrence, which recur quite regularly as a property of texts in general. Thus certain items tend to keep company, or **collocate**, with others: there is, at it were, a kind of mutual attraction that draws them together. So the word *unforeseen* will attract the word *circumstances*, *foregone* will attract *conclusion*, *crying* will attract *shame* and *pious* will attract *hope*, and so on. But **collocation** goes beyond the relationship between two lexical items in a noun phrase to include many other recurring combinations in phrases like: *as a matter of fact, all things considered, when all's said and done, all things being equal, for better or for worse*, and so on. Such **formulaic phrases** are easy enough for proficient speakers of English to cite: they are aware of them as familiar idiomatic features of their usage, and no corpus analysis is needed to reveal them. But there are innumerable other textual patterns and phrases that emerge from corpus analysis that the language user is not aware of. It is easy enough to demonstrate this by means of a **concordance**, which displays all the occurrences of a particular word in lines of text so that one can see at a glance where co-textual combinations recur. Concordances for words which are semantically related can be compared and their collocational differences identified. For example, the words *big* and *large*, *little* and *small* (already mentioned in Chapter 2) are shown not only to occur with different overall frequencies, but to have rather different collocational preferences. Similarly, it turns out that the words *amazing*, *astonishing*, and *surprising* not only vary considerably in frequency but also in the way they can combine with other words in lexical phrases or bundles. Thus the last of these often occurs in the phrase: *it is not surprising that ...*, whereas the others do not. *It is not amazing that ...* and *it is not astonishing that ...*, though possible constructions in English (in the Hymes sense), seem hardly to occur in attested usage.

What corpus analysis reveals is that the constituents of texts are not so much separate words and structures as patterns of language, collocations and lexical bundles, of variable flexibility. This suggests that producing a text is, to some extent at least, a matter of assembling it from pre-fabricated parts, making whatever adjustments are necessary—changing a word here, a structure there as co-textually required. This is clearly a more efficient process than composing a text bit by linguistic bit, and knowledge of this process must be part of our communicative competence. So, in reference again to Hymes, what is actually performed relates to what is feasible. The use of recurring patterns of language, stored ready for use in the mind, is in this case motivated by the co-operative principle. To deliberately disregard them would be to violate the manner maxim.

Semantic prosodies

But what motivates the use of *particular* collocational combinations? In some cases we might suggest that if there is any motivation at all, it is only to signal membership of a particular community by conforming to its customary idiom. In other cases, a collocation may be explained by reference to general semantic principles. Take the example of the phrase mentioned earlier: *it is not surprising that* ... Why is it that it is normal for *surprising* to occur in this combination but not *amazing* or *astonishing*? One answer might be that it is simply a matter of custom, a kind of ingrained habit and that's that. Alternatively we could look at whether there is anything in the semantic meaning of these words which might explain this collocational constraint. Further consultation of the concordance lines would reveal that *surprising* is also often preceded by the intensifier *very*, but the other words are not. The reason for this, we could conclude, is that intensity is already a semantic feature of *amazing* and *astonishing*. We might then propose the general rule that words which are marked for intensity do not normally combine with *very* or appear in the frame *it is not—that,* whereas words unmarked for intensity, like *surprising*, do. Or take the verb *cause*. A glance at a concordance display will show that its normal collocates are words which denote disagreeable things, like *pain*, *disease*, *distress*, *disruption*, and so on. It is therefore said to have a *negative* **semantic prosody**. In contrast, the verb *bring about* has a *positive* semantic prosody in that its typical collocates are words like *improvement*, *cure*, *solution*, *success*. Thus a problem is caused but a solution is brought about.

In these cases, then, we can explain particular collocational combinations in texts by identifying the more general semantic properties of the words concerned. We need to note that these have to do with tendencies and probabilities. The essential point is that these are the default meanings of the words—meanings that they would normally be expected to have—and that any departure from the norm is likely to be noticed, with the likely consequence, yet again, that implicatures will arise. So if we come across a reference to a solution that has been caused, or a problem that has been brought about, and if we have reason to believe that the selection of words is deliberate, we are likely to interpret them as indicating irony, or some other attitude, on the part of the author.

With reference to the two kinds of knowledge referred to in Chapter 6, these semantic prosodies can be said to be part of systemic knowledge. There are other collocational patterns that, like certain word frequencies as mentioned earlier, can be related to schematic knowledge in that they can be said to represent the way reality is conceptually constructed by a community of language users. If, for example, (to return briefly to the text fragments we looked at earlier) we were to call up a concordance for the words *refugees* or *police* as they occur in a corpus of newspaper texts, the collocations they enter into could be said to indicate how refugees and the police are conceptually represented in the press. A comparison of concordances from the corpora of different newspapers, or of different domains of use altogether, might indicate degrees of schematic generality—the extent to which the collocations reflect a particular or more general set of cultural assumptions.

Conclusion: text analysis and discourse interpretation

So, to take up the question raised at the end of the last chapter, how far does text analysis contribute to an understanding of the discourse process and enable us to assign communicative significance to what is said or written? As we have seen, the computer analysis of corpora provides us with profiles of the occurrence and co-occurrence of textual features and these serve as a norm of what is customary against which any particular instance of usage can be compared. Where there is deviation from the norm, and therefore a departure from what is expected, this is likely to be taken as acting contrary to the co-operative principle and will create an implicature—there is some under-lying significance here, some effect intended beyond what is actually said.

Just what this significance may be, however, is a different matter. And here, in this last chapter, we return to the points made in the first about the nature of language in use and the distinction between text and discourse. Textual analysis can only tell us about texts, the language that people produce (or more strictly, have produced) in the process of communication. It cannot tell us about the process itself, about how people negotiate a relationship between text and context in order to bring about a degree of discourse convergence appropriate to their purpose. As we have seen, what people intend to mean by the texts they produce, and what they are interpreted as meaning, cannot be directly inferred from the texts themselves, no matter how precisely these are analysed. For texts only have reality for the language user as a means to an end, as a way of mediating discourse, and they are not normally produced as an end in themselves. But they can, of course, be *analysed* as an end in themselves, and this is what corpus analysis so effectively does. The result is a wealth of new information about how texts are constructed. These textual facts cannot account for all the other factors we have considered in this book that come into play in making meaning, and it would be a mistake to claim that they can. But what they can do is to alert us to possible intentions and interpretations which we might otherwise not be aware of, and so provide a basis, and a stimulus, for further empirical enquiry into the pragmatics of discourse and the nature of human communication.

SECTION 2
Readings

Chapter 1
Language in use

Text 1
WILLIAM LABOV: *The Study of Nonstandard English.*
National Council of Teachers of English 1969, pages 54–5

This short text and the one that follows give definitions of discourse, but from different points of view. Labov opposed the formalist approach to linguistic description which was dominant at the time by insisting that linguistics should be the study of language in its social context, which involved going beyond linguistic categories to what he calls here Type I rules that underlie actions using language.

Commands and refusals are actions; declarations, interrogatives, imperatives are linguistic categories—things that are said, rather than things that are done. The rules we need will show how things are done with words and how one interprets these utterances as actions: in other words, relating what is done to what is said and what is said to what is done. This area of linguistics can be called 'discourse analysis'; but it is not well known or developed. Linguistic theory is not yet rich enough to write such rules, for one must take into account such sociological, non-linguistic categories as roles, rights and obligations. What small progress has been made in this area is the work of sociologists and philosophers who are investigating informally the Type I rules which lie behind everyday 'common sense' behavior.

▷ *How far do you think Labov's distinction here between what is said and what is done fits in with what is said in Chapter 1 about the difference between sentence and text?*

▷ *Can you suggest why sociological categories like roles, rights, and obligations are needed to study language in use?*

Text 2

WALLACE CHAFE: 'Discourse: Overview',
in *International Encyclopedia of Linguistics*, 2nd edn.
Oxford University Press 2005, pages 439–40

According to this encyclopedia entry, most scholars make no distinction between the concepts of text and discourse, and use both terms to refer to a unit of language above the sentence.

The term *discourse* is used in somewhat different ways by different scholars, but underlying the differences is a common concern for language beyond the boundaries of isolated sentences. The term *text* is used in similar ways. Both terms may refer to a unit of language larger than the sentence: one may speak of 'a discourse' or 'a text.' 'Discourse' may also refer to the study of such a unit, a branch of linguistics coordinate with morphology or syntax. One may speak of a linguist who specializes in discourse, for example. Often the terms discourse (or text) analysis, or discourse (or text) linguistics, are used in this way.

▷ *Do you think Chafe's statement here is consistent with the account of text and discourse given in Chapter 1?*

▷ *How far do you think Labov's view of discourse in Text 1 shows 'the common concern for language beyond the isolated sentence'?*

Text 3

GUY COOK: *The Discourse of Advertising*, 2nd edn.
Routledge 2001, page 71

In spoken communication, meanings are not just expressed in the language of the text but by paralanguage—gesture, tone of voice, and other forms of behaviour. The size, shape, and positioning of signs in written language use can also be used as paralinguistic devices for indicating meaning.

In communication, language always has a physical substance of some kind, and though this substance—sound waves or marks on paper—serves as a trigger for the assignment of phonemes and graphemes by the receiver, allowing him or her to build the signs which create linguistic meaning, it carries other kinds of meaning too. In face-to-face communication, important meanings may be conveyed by eye contact, gesture, body movement, clothing, touch, body position, physical proximity, voice quality, volume, pitch range and laughter; in writing, the same is true of page and letter sizes, fonts and handwriting styles. These and many other factors also carry meaning which may reinforce or contradict the linguistic meaning of the signs which they accompany. They are examples of paralanguage.

It is not enough to say, as some linguists do, that such behaviour is best understood as another semiotic system, separate from language. Firstly, the two modes of meaning are not separate. Paralanguage interacts with language and on occasion outweighs it. (To see that this is true, one has only to imagine the effect of someone sobbing while saying: 'I am not upset'.) There is a good deal of experimental psychological evidence to support this view of the power of paralanguage.

▷ *Can you think of examples of where the different kinds of paralanguage—eye contact, gesture, body movement and so on—affect the meaning of what is said?*

▷ *'These and many other factors also carry meaning.' Can you think of factors other than those mentioned that carry meaning in spoken and written language use?*

▷ *How do the points made in this text relate to Labov's distinction in Text 1 between what is said and what is done?*

Text 4

GILLIAN BROWN and GEORGE YULE: *Discourse Analysis.* Cambridge University Press 1983, pages 11–12

This text discusses the relationship between what the producer of a text intends to mean by it, and how it is interpreted.

It is suggested that this is particularly problematic in the case of spoken language.

It must be emphasised that, however objective the notion of 'text' may appear as we have defined it ('the verbal record of a communicative act'), the perception and interpretation of each text is essentially subjective. Different individuals pay attention to different aspects of texts. The content of a text appeals to them or fits into their experience differently. In discussing texts we idealise away from this variability of the experiencing of the text and assume what Schutz has called 'the reciprocity of perspectives', whereby we take it for granted that readers of a text or listeners to a text share the same experience (Schutz, 1953). Clearly for a great deal of ordinary everyday language this assumption of an amount of overlap of point of view sufficient to allow mutual comprehension is necessary. From time to time, however, we are brought to a halt by different interpretations of 'the same text'. This is particularly the case when critical attention is being focussed on details of spoken language which were only ever intended by the speaker or ephemeral parts, relatively unimportant, of the working-out of what he wanted to say. It seems fair to suggest that discourse analysis of spoken language is particularly prone to over-analysis. A text frequently has a much wider variety of interpretations imposed upon it by analysts studying it at their leisure, than would ever have been possible for the participants in the communicative interaction which gives rise to the 'text'. Once the analyst has 'created' a written transcription from a recorded spoken version, the written text is available to him in just the way a literary text is available to the literary critic. It is important to remember, when we discuss spoken 'texts', the transitoriness of the original.

▷ Both this text and Text 3 discuss problems that arise in the interpretation of spoken language. Are the two texts in agreement?

▷ At times here the word 'text' appears in inverted commas, but at other times it does not. Can you explain why?

Chapter 2
Communication

Text 5

D. H. HYMES: 'On communicative competence',
in J. B. Pride and Janet Holmes (eds.): *Sociolinguistics*.
Penguin Books 1972, pages 281–2

*In this often-quoted passage, Hymes talks about the kinds of
judgement that somebody competent in a language is able to
make about a sample of it. In Chomsky's linguistic theory,
prevalent at the time, two kinds of judgement could be made:
how far the sample was grammatical as a sentence and how
far is was acceptable as a use of language. Hymes suggests that
we need to take not two but four kinds of judgement into
account.*

If an adequate theory of language users and language use is to be
developed, it seems that judgements must be recognized to be in
fact not of two kinds but of four. And if linguistic theory is to be
integrated with theory of communication and culture, this
fourfold distinction must be stated in a sufficiently generalized
way. I would suggest, then, that for language and other forms of
communication (culture), four questions arise:

1 Whether (and to what degree) something is formally possible;
2 Whether (and to what degree) something is feasible in virtue of
  the means of implementation available;
3 Whether (and to what degree) something is appropriate
  (adequate, happy, successful) in relation to the context in
  which it is used and evaluated;
4 Whether (and to what degree) something is in fact done,
  actually performed, and what its doing entails.

A linguistic illustration: a sentence may be grammatical, awkward,
tactful and rare. (One might think of the four as successive subjects; more likely they should be pictured as overlapping circles.)

▷ *Hymes gives one linguistic illustration. Can you provide more
  —giving samples, from English or any other language—that
  are possible but not appropriate, possible but not actually
  performed, and so on?*

> *Hymes says these questions apply to 'other forms of commu-
> nication' as well as language. Can you think of examples?*

> *'... more likely they should be pictured as overlapping circles.'
> Can you suggest why?*

Text 6

JOHN SEARLE: *Speech Acts*. Cambridge University Press
1969, pages 22–4

*The book from which this text is taken looks at language in
use from a philosophical point of view. The theory of speech
acts that it proposes has had enormous influence on the study
of discourse.*

Imagine a speaker and a hearer and suppose that in appropriate
circumstances the speaker utters one of the following sentences:

1 Sam smokes habitually.
2 Does Sam smoke habitually?
3 Sam, smoke habitually!
4 Would that Sam smoked habitually.

Now let us ask how we might characterize or describe the
speaker's utterance of one of these. What shall we say the speaker
is doing when he utters one of these?

One thing is obvious: anyone who utters one of these can be
said to have uttered a sentence formed of words in the English
language. But clearly this is only the beginning of a description,
for the speaker in uttering one of these is characteristically saying
something and not merely mouthing words. In uttering 1 a
speaker is making (what philosophers call) an assertion, in 2
asking a question, in 3 giving an order, and in 4 (a somewhat
archaic form) expressing a wish or desire. And in the performance
of each of these four different acts the speaker performs certain
other acts which are common to all four: in uttering any of these
the speaker *refers to* or mentions or designates a certain object
Sam, and he predicates the expression 'smokes habitually' (or one
of its inflections) of the object referred to. Thus we shall say that
in the utterance of all four the reference and predication are the
same, though in each case the same reference and predication
occur as part of a complete speech act which is different from any

of the other three. We thus detach the notions of referring and predicating from the notions of such complete speech acts as asserting, questioning, commanding, etc ....

The first upshot of our preliminary reflections, then, is that in the utterance of any of the four sentences in the example a speaker is characteristically performing at least three distinct kinds of acts. a) The uttering of words (morphemes, sentences); b) referring and predicating; c) stating, questioning, commanding, promising etc.

Let us assign names to these under the general heading of speech acts:

a) Uttering words (morphemes, sentences) = performing *utterance acts*.
b) Referring and predicating = performing *propositional acts*.
c) Stating, questioning, commanding, promising, etc. = performing *illocutionary acts*.

▷ *How far do you think this text can be read as a continuation of Text 1 in that it explores the relationship between what is said and what is done? Are Labov and Searle in agreement?*

▷ *Searle talks about performing 'at least three distinct kinds of acts' at the same time. Do you think it is possible to perform one or two of these acts on their own—can you perform an utterance act without expressing a proposition, for example, or express a proposition without performing an illocutionary act?*

Chapter 3
Context

Text 7
MICHAEL STUBBS: *Text and Corpus Analysis.*
Blackwell 1966, page 6

Here Stubbs takes up the issue already touched on in Text 4 about how far meaning can be said to be in a text, and how far it is a matter of variable interpretation, dependent on a range of contextual factors. Some meanings, Stubbs suggests, are more contextually dependent than others.

A problem which crops up in various forms is: where is the meaning of a text located? Is the meaning inside the text itself? Or inside the mind of the person who makes sense of it? Or is it in the speech community somewhere—perhaps in the form of a consensus interpretation on which we could all agree?

Suppose I receive a legal document, which I read but do not fully understand. I might ring up a friend who is a lawyer and read a problematic sentence over the phone. My friend might then explain to me what this sentence means. I will have read it, but the lawyer will have interpreted it. So was the meaning in the text? Possibly, though it seems to require the knowledge of the lawyer to get the meaning out. And note the ambiguity of the word *read*. It sometimes refers merely to the words on the page: I have read a sentence aloud over the telephone. And it sometimes means 'read and understand', as when I say I have read a good book on holiday.

Here is a very simple model of the relation between text and context. In common sense terms, it seems clear that the meaning of a text depends on at least three things: the language of the text itself, who produced it and who is responding to it. By the language itself I mean the words actually spoken or written, and their patterns of lexical collocations and syntactic and rhetorical structures. Some meanings are created by the words themselves and their observable interrelationships. ... But some meanings depend on our knowledge of the point of view of the author. We may interpret things quite differently, depending on when and where and by whom the language is produced—for example, depending on the status or authority of the speaker or writer: a person in the street, an expert, a government minister, a government committee, an author of a school textbook, a judge summing up in court and so on. And some meanings are brought to the text by readers and listeners: according to their specialist knowledge, their cultural assumptions or their familiarity with other related texts. Readers and listeners also have different points of view, and respond to texts in different ways.

▷ *Do you think that the points about text interpretation here support the statement in Text 4 that 'the perception and interpretation of each text is essentially subjective'?*

▷ *Explain how the 'very simple model' that Stubbs proposes might apply to his own example about the reading of a legal document.*

▷ *'Some meanings are created by the words themselves ... some meanings depend on when and where and by whom the language is produced ... some meanings are brought to the text by readers and listeners'. Can you suggest examples of these different kinds of meaning?*

Text 8
BRONISLAW MALINOWSKI: 'The Problem of Meaning in Primitive Languages', supplement to C. K. Ogden and I. A. Richards, *The Meaning of Meaning*. Routledge & Kegan Paul 1936, pages 306–7

Malinowski was an anthropologist and recognized that in the communities he studied, language was essentially a mode of social action and so could only be understood in relation to the context of situation and the broader context of culture in which it was used. Here he is referring to an example of language used by the Trobriand islanders in the western Pacific.

Returning once more to our native utterance, it needs no special stressing that in a primitive language the meaning of any single word is to a very high degree dependent on its context. The words 'wood', 'paddle', 'place' had to be translated in the free interpretation in order to show what is their real meaning, conveyed to a native by the context in which they appear. Again, it is equally clear that the meaning of the expression 'we arrive near the village (of our destination)' literally: 'we paddle in place', is determined only by taking it in the context of the whole utterance. This latter again, becomes only intelligible when it is placed within its *context of situation*, if I may be allowed to coin an expression which indicates on the one hand that the concept of *context* has to be broadened and on the other that the *situation* in which words are uttered can never be passed over as irrelevant to the linguistic expression. We see how the conception of context must be substantially widened, if it is to furnish us with its full utility. In fact it must burst the bonds of mere linguistics and be carried over into the analysis of the general conditions under which a language is spoken. Thus, starting from the wider idea of context, we arrive once more at the results of the foregoing section, namely that the study of any language, spoken by a people who live under conditions different from our own and possess a different culture, must be carried out in conjunction with the study of their culture and their environment.

▷ *'The conception of context must be substantially widened'. But what exactly do you understand this wider context to consist of?*

▷ *How far do the ideas here correspond with the 'simple model' of text and context proposed by Stubbs in Text 7?*

▷ *Malinowski talks here specifically about the spoken use of 'primitive' languages. Do you think his notion of context of situation applies equally to all uses of all languages?*

Text 9

JAMES PAUL GEE: *An Introduction to Discourse Analysis: Theory and Method*. Routledge 1999, pages 62–3

In emphasizing the importance of the cultural context, this text echoes the ideas, and even the wording, of the preceding text, written over sixty years earlier—a salutary reminder that in this field of study at least, a text that is dated is not always out of date. Gee illustrates the particular difficulties of relating what is said to what is done (see Text 1) when dealing with the discourse of a different culture. The example he takes is from the Mayan people of Yucatán in Mexico, adapted, as Gee acknowledges, from the book 'Language and Communicative Practices' by William Hanks (1996).

When we watch language-in-action in a culture quite different from our own, even simple interactions can be inexplicable, thanks to the fact that we do not know many of the cultural models at play. This means that even if we can figure out the situated meaning of some words, we cannot see any sense to why these situated meanings have arisen (why they were assembled here and now). So let's move, with Hanks, to Yucatan, Mexico.

In a small town in Yucatan, a Mayan Shaman named 'Don Chabo' is sharing a meal with his daughter-in-law, Margot, and a visiting anthropologist. A young man, named 'Yuum', approaches from the outside, and, standing at the window, asks: 'Is Don Chabo seated?' Margot replies: 'Go over there. He's drinking. Go over there inside.' These are about as simple as sentences get.

And yet the meaning of these sentences is not so straight-forward after all. For example, the people seated around the table are having a meal, so why does Margot say that Don Chabo is drinking? Furthermore, Margot's response implies that Don Chabo is drinking, despite the fact that he was, at that moment, gazing off into space with a roll in his hand. Indeed in Mayan, it would have been equally true here to say Don Chabo was 'drinking' had he been altogether done with (eating) his meal.

Margot's response implies, as well, that Don Chabo was 'seated.' Yet, it turns out, it would have been equally true to say that he was seated had he been standing or even off somewhere else, even taking a bath in his own home.

Or, to take one final example, Margot uses the Mayan word for 'there' that means 'maximally distant from the speaker,' the same word people in Yucatan use for relatives who live outside Yucatan, in other states in the Mexican Republic. She does this despite the fact she is telling Yuum to go into her father-in-law's house, not 10 meters away from hers and within the same compound as her house.

How can it be that people can be drinking when they are eating or doing nothing at all? That they are seated when they are standing or taking a bath? That they are far distant from something 10 meters away? ...

▷ *Think of what cultural factors might be at work here, and try to come up with possible answers to these questions before going on to the continuation of Gee's text, which provides an explanation.*

Things work out in this way because Mayans (these Mayans, in any case), though they almost always take food with drink and vice versa, use the words 'drink' and 'eat' against a cultural model of meals in terms of which their morning and evening meals are 'drinking' and their larger main meal in the midafternoon is 'eating.' Furthermore, to these Mayans, as long as the social engagement of mealtime still goes on, regardless of whether the 'meal' itself is finished or not, a person is still 'drinking' or 'eating.'

Many Mayans live in walled compounds that contain several houses. Their cultural models for house and home are, thus, rather different from (some of) ours. They use the word 'seated' to mean that one is 'at home' and available, regardless of where one is in the compound ...

Finally, Mayans have their own cultural models, as all of us do, of how physical and social space work and are related. Margot is excluded from her father-in-law's house, unless she has a specific reason to be there, for social reasons having to do with Mayan cultural models of social relationships and spaces within homes. Thus she uses the word for 'far distant' due to social rather than physical distance.

▷ *Can you give examples from your own culture, or other cultures you are familiar with, that would serve as further illustration of Gee's point?*

▷ *This example of 'language-in-action' is taken from 'a culture quite different from our own'. Could similar problems arise within the same culture?*

▷ *The 'language-in-action' discussed here is not the original Mayan of Margot's utterance, but a literal translation into English. Do you think this affects the points being made in any way?*

▷ *Refer to pages 23–4 in Chapter 4, where Bartlett's experiments reveal similar problems in cross-cultural understanding. Bartlett uses the term 'schema' to account for them. Do you think Gee's 'cultural model' is just an alternative term for the same thing, or is he saying something different?*

Text 10

DAN SPERBER and DIERDRE WILSON:
Relevance: Communication and Cognition, 2nd edn.
Blackwell 1995, pages 15–16

The previous two texts have dealt with context from a socio-cultural point of view. This one looks at the concept from a philosophical perspective.

The set of premises used in interpreting an utterance (apart from the premise that the utterance in question has been produced) constitutes what is generally known as the *context*. A context is a psychological construct, a subset of the hearer's assumptions about the world. It is these assumptions, of course, rather than the actual state of the world, that affect the interpretation of an utterance. A context in this sense is not limited to information about the immediate physical environment or the immediately preceding utterances: expectations about the future, scientific hypotheses or religious beliefs, anecdotal memories, general cultural assumptions, beliefs about the mental state of the speaker, may all play a role in interpretation.

While it is clear that members of the same linguistic community converge on the same language, and plausible that they converge on the same inferential abilities, the same is not true of their assumptions about the world. True, all humans are constrained by their species-specific cognitive abilities in developing their representation of the world, and members of the same cultural group share a number of experiences, teachings and views. However, beyond this common framework, individuals tend to be highly idiosyncratic. Differences in life history necessarily lead to differences in memorised information. Moreover, it has been repeatedly shown that two people witnessing the same event—even a salient and highly memorable event like a car accident—may construct dramatically different representations of it, disagreeing not just on their interpretation of it, but in their memory of the basic physical facts. While grammars neutralise the differences between dissimilar experiences, cognition and memory superimpose differences even on common experiences.

▷ *How far do you think the notion of context as expressed here corresponds with that outlined by Stubbs in Text 7?*

▷ *The suggestion here is that context as a psychological construct is different for each individual. If so, can there ever be an agreement about the interpretation of an utterance?*

▷ *In Text 9, Gee explains the meaning of an utterance by referring to what he calls a 'cultural model'. In this text, 'general cultural assumptions' are said to be only one aspect of context. Is there a basic disagreement here? What comment do you think Sperber and Wilson might make on what Gee has to say?*

Chapter 4
Schematic conventions

Text 11

WILLIAM LABOV: *Sociolinguistic Patterns*. Basil Blackwell 1972, pages 252–4

Labov here deals with what in Chapter 4 (page 29) is referred to as an interpersonal schema, in that he seeks to establish the rules that people follow in turn-taking so that 'one utterance follows another in a rational rule-governed manner.'

The question is: how much and what kind of data do we need in order to form sound judgments and interpret sequences of utterances as the participants in the conversation do? The simplest case is that of elliptical responses, as in 36.

36 A: Are you going to work tomorrow?
B: Yes.

Here our normal knowledge of English syntax is sufficient to allow us to derive B's utterance from *Yes, I am going to work tomorrow*. There is a simple rule of discourse of the following form:

37 If A utters a question of the form Q-S_1, and B responds with an existential E (including *yes, no, probably, maybe,* etc.), then B is heard as answering A with the statement E-S_1.

But now let us consider sequences of the following form:

38 A: She never helps at home.
B: Yes.

39 A: She told you what we are interested in.
    B: Yes.

40 A: You live on 115th St.
    B: No. I live on 116th.

We encounter many such examples in our analyses of therapeutic interviews and in everyday speech. Rule 37 obviously does not apply: there is no Q-S$_1$ in the A form. Is it true that any statement can followed with a *yes* or *no*? The following sequences seem to indicate the opposite.

41 A: I don't like the way you said that.
    B: *Yes.

42 A: I feel hot today.
    B: *No.

It is not only that 41–42 do not require or tolerate a *yes* or *no* answer, but even more strikingly that statements like 37–40 seem to demand such a response. We find many cases where speakers will not let a conversation continue unless a *yes* or *no* answer is given to such statements. The rule which operates here is one of the simplest invariant rules of discourse. Given two parties in a conversation, A and B, we can distinguish as 'A-events' the things that A knows about but B does not; as 'B-events' the things that B knows but A does not; and as 'AB-events' knowledge which is shared equally by A and B. The rule then states:

43 If A makes a statement about a B-event, it is heard as a request for confirmation.

▷ *Explain how this rule applies to the examples 38–41, and provide further examples of your own of how the rule operates.*

▷ *43 is said to be an 'invariant rule of discourse'. Is it really invariant? Is it always the case, whatever the language or context, that if A makes a statement about a B-event it will always be heard as a request for confirmation?*

Text 12

A. J. SANFORD and S. C. GARROD: *Understanding Written Language*. John Wiley & Sons 1981, pages 8–10

Whereas the preceding text was concerned with the operation of interpersonal schemata in conversation, this one deals with ideational schemata in written language use.

The basis on which discourse is produced and understood is essentially contractual. A writer wishes to convey an idea to his readers. In essence, this means that he must establish in the mind of his reader a situational model which is the same as (or closely similar to) the one in his own mind. He can then refer to this model as his discourse unfolds and be reasonably certain what he ways will be intelligible. In the absence of such a common model, a discourse will be unintelligible, even if every sentence in it is coherent and grammatical. ...

Consider the following example:

(11) John Smith got ready to go to the theatre.
(11′) He tied his hair into a top-knot with a huge velvet bow.

(11′) seems strange. It does not fit the idea of a man going to the theatre. However, it would pass as reasonable if the discourse had been preceded by an orienting statement:

(12) John Smith was playing the 'old dame' in the small-town pantomime.

The point with this last example is that while it is intelligible, it is awkward in the extreme. Readers may have had various theories about it:

– It doesn't make sense.
– John is going to a fancy-dress ball at the theatre.
– John is a transvestite.
– The bow is part of his costume.

In the absence of a thematic model, no interpretation is possible.

These examples illustrate what happens when a writer fails to honour his part of the contract. For the reader's part, his problem is somewhat different: he has to assume that the writer is in fact writing about a coherent situation and that it is his task to discover what this situation is. The utility of the mental model which we suggest the reader generates is that it will allow for unique representations of what is being said. While any sentence may be ambiguous in isolation, once it is interpreted with respect to a particular scenario it takes on a unique meaning.

▷ *As in Text 9, reference is made here to a model, described as 'situational', 'common', 'thematic', and 'mental'. Do you take this to be an alternative term for 'schema' or do you think the term means something different?*

▷ *'In the absence of a thematic model, no interpretation is possible.' Is this always the case? And does the model also have to be common for interpretation to take place?*

▷ *How far do examples given here and the 'various theories' readers might have about them illustrate the working of the cultural model as discussed in Text 9?*

Text 13
MICHAEL HOEY: *Textual Interaction: An Introduction to Written Discourse Analysis.* Routledge 2001, pages 120–2

This text is also about the schemata (or scripts—an alternative term) of written language, but Hoey argues that their value for analysis is limited because they are elusive of exact definition. He suggests we should think of a more general set of expectations which are triggered by particular words and are common across a wide schematic range.

Revealing though concepts such as schema and script are for a general understanding of the writing and reading processes, they are of limited value in text analysis or in the teaching of reading or writing. This is because there appears to be no practical limit to the number of schemata or scripts we can hold and the exact content and boundaries of each schema or script are open to real question. It is no accident that the restaurant script is so often cited—it happens to be an unusually self-contained and bounded set of knowledge and expectations. Furthermore, even if these problems were solvable in principle, we would still never in practice be able to list, let alone describe, all the schemata/scripts that a reader develops in his or her life or that a writer is capable of making use of. In short, schemata and scripts are not practicable analytic tools. What we need is something that allows us to generalise about these schemata/scripts without losing the insight that readers co-operate with writers in making a common meaning.

The answer in part lies in the fact that readers seem to bring two kinds of knowledge to bear on the texts they read—the specific knowledge described by schemata and scripts and a more generalised set of expectations that are shared across a range of texts. If we look again at Shank and Abelson's incomplete minitext [i.e. John knew his wife's operation would be expensive. There was always Uncle Harry. John reached for the telephone book], we can see that the question that the reader is likely to ask on being told that *John knew his wife's operation would be expensive* is *What did he do about it?* In other words, the reader will recognise the situation described in the first sentence as a problematic one and will expect a response to the problem described. This would have been true even if no specific schema could be activated. Thus the sentence:

7.4 John knew the gill net would be expensive

is extremely unlikely to trigger any schema in your mind, unless you happen to be keen on fishing (a gill net being a net that is suspended in water as a way of trapping fish by the gills). Yet the more generalised expectation would be as strong here as it was when the expensive item was an operation. Just as the word *operation* triggers the schema of hospitals, welfare systems and so on, so the word *expensive* triggers a 'generalised script' of problem followed by attempt at solution.

▷ Hoey talks about 'the specific knowledge described by schemata and scripts'. Does schematic knowledge have to be specific?

▷ The concepts of schema and script are said to be 'of limited value in text analysis or in the teaching of reading or writing'. What reasons are there for supposing that the 'generalised script' that Hoey proposes would be of greater value?

Chapter 5
Co-textual relations

Text 14

M. A. K. HALLIDAY and RUQUAIYA HASAN: *Cohesion in English*. Longman 1976, pages 10–11

This text discusses cohesion as the setting up of meaning relations across sentences by means of a set of linguistic devices which links sentences together, thereby creating what the authors refer to as 'texture'.

To say that two sentences cohere by virtue of relations in their meaning is not by itself very precise. Practically any two sentences might be shown to have something to do with each other as far as their meaning is concerned; and although in judging whether there is texture or not we certainly have recourse to some feeling about how much the sentences do actually inter-relate in meaning, we could not give any very explicit account of the degree of relatedness that is needed or how it is to be measured.

But there is one specific kind of meaning relation that is critical for the creation of texture: that in which ONE ELEMENT IS INTERPRETED BY REFERENCE TO ANOTHER. What cohesion has to do with is the way in which the meaning of the elements is interpreted. Where the interpretation of any item in the discourse requires making reference to some other item in the discourse, there is cohesion.

Consider the example

[1:14] He said so.

This sentence is perfectly intelligible as it stands; we know what it means in the sense that we can 'decode' it semantically. But it is UNINTERPRETABLE because we do not know who 'he' is or what he said. For this we have to refer elsewhere, to its 'context' in the sense of what has gone before.

Now it is also true that, given just the sentence

[1:15] John said everything.

we do not know who 'John' is, or what he said, either. But there is an important difference between examples [1:14] and [1:15]. In

[1:14], the items *he* and *so* contain in their meaning an explicit signal that the means of their interpretation is available somewhere in the environment. Hearing or reading this sentence, we know that it links up with some other passage in which there is an indication of who 'he' is and what he said. This is the not the case with *John* or *everything*, neither of which necessarily presupposes any such source of further information.

▷ *Reference is made here to 'context' and 'environment'. What do you think is meant by these terms?*

▷ *The authors of this text and that of Text 9 are concerned with interpretation. Are they talking about the same thing?*

▷ *How would you comment on the way cohesion is defined here by reference to these two sentences referred to by Hoey in Text 13:*

John knew his wife's operation would be expensive. There was always Uncle Harry.

▷ *Is there a cohesive link between these sentences? If not, how do they cohere?*

Chapter 6
The negotiation of meaning

Text 15
H. P. GRICE: 'Logic and Conversation', in Peter Cole and Jerry L. Morgan (eds.) *Syntax and Semantics*, vol. 3, *Speech Acts*. Academic Press 1975, pages 45–6

This is an extract from Grice's formulation of the co-operative principle. The original paper reads as more tentative and provisional than do the second-hand versions of it that are usually provided in the literature.

We might then formulate a rough general principle which participants will be expected (ceteris paribus) to observe, namely: Make your conversational contribution such as is required, at the stage at which it occurs, by the accepted purpose or direction of the talk exchange in which you are engaged. One might label this the COOPERATIVE PRINCIPLE.

On the assumption that some such general principle as this is acceptable, one may perhaps distinguish four categories under one or another of which will fall certain more specific maxims and sub-maxims, the following of which will, in general, yield results in accordance with the Cooperative Principle. Echoing Kant, I call these categories Quantity, Quality, Relation, and Manner. The category of QUANTITY relates to the quantity of information to be provided, and under it fall the following maxims:

1 Make your contribution as informative as is required (for the current purposes of the exchange).
2 Do not make your contribution more informative than is required. ...

Under the category of QUALITY falls a supermaxim—'Try to make your contribution one that is true'—and two more specific maxims:

1 Do not say what you believe to be false.
2 Do not say that for which you lack adequate evidence.

Under the category of RELATION I place a single maxim, namely, 'Be relevant.' Though the maxim itself is terse, its formulation conceals a number of problems that exercise me a good deal: questions about what different kinds and focuses of relevance there may be, and how these shift in the course of a talk exchange, how to allow for the fact that subjects of conversation are legitimately changed, and so on. I find the treatment of these questions exceedingly difficult, and I hope to revert to them in a later work.

Finally, under the category of MANNER, which I understand as relating not (like the previous categories) to what is said but, rather, to HOW what is said is said, I include the supermaxim—'Be perspicuous'—and various maxims such as:

1 Avoid obscurity of expression.
2 Avoid ambiguity.
3 Be brief (avoid unnecessary prolixity).
4 Be orderly.

And one might need others.

▷ *Grice says that he finds the Relation maxim problematic. Why do you think it should be more problematic than the others?*

▷ *In the first of the Quantity maxims, Grice adds the rider '(for the current purposes of the exchange)'. Does this only apply to this maxim or should it apply to all the others as well?*

▷ *Why do you think 'Be brief ' is categorized as a maxim of Manner rather than of Quantity?*

▷ *'And one might need others.' Can you think of any other maxims that might be added?*

Text 16

STEPHEN C. LEVINSON: *Pragmatics.*
Cambridge University Press 1983, page 103

In discussing Grice's maxims, Levinson here raises the interesting question of how far concepts that are proposed specifically to explain how language is used might apply to human behaviour in general. This would not only apply to the co-operative principle, but to notions like the least effort principle and territoriality (see Chapter 6).

But what is the source of these maxims of conversational behaviour? Are they conventional rules that we learn as we learn, say, table manners? Grice suggests that the maxims are in fact not arbitrary conventions, but rather describe rational means for conducting co-operative exchanges. If this is so, we would expect them to govern aspects of non-linguistic behaviour too, and indeed they seem to do so. Consider, for example, a situation in which A and B are fixing a car. If the maxim of Quality is interpreted as the injunction to produce non-spurious or sincere acts (a move we need to make anyway to extend the maxim to questions, promises, invitations, etc.), B would fail to comply with this if, when asked for brake fluid, he knowingly passes A the oil, or when asked to tighten up the bolts on the steering column he merely pretends to do so. Similarly, A would fail to observe the maxim of Quantity, the injunction to make one's contribution in the right proportion, if, when B needs three bolts, he purposely passes him only one, or alternatively passes him 300. Likewise with Relevance: if B wants three bolts, he wants them *now* not half an hour later. Finally, B would fail to comply with the maxim of Manner, enjoining clarity of purpose, if, when A needs a bolt of size 8, B passes him the bolt in a box that usually contains bolts of size 10. In each of these cases the behaviour falls short of some natural notion of full co-operation, because it violates one or another of the non-verbal analogues of the maxims of conversation. This suggests that the maxims do indeed derive from general considerations of rationality applicable to all kinds of co-operative exchanges, and if so they ought in addition to have universal application, at least to the extent that other, culture specific, constraints on interaction allow. Broadly, this too seems to be so.

▷ *Can you think of other situations where the maxims would apply to non-linguistic behaviour?*

▷ *What leads Levinson to the conclusion that the maxims 'ought to have universal application'? Do you accept his argument?*

▷ *He adds the proviso ' to the extent that other, culture-specific, constraints on interaction allow'. What does he mean by this? Can you suggest any such culture-specific constraints on the operation of the maxims?*

Chapter 7
Critical analysis

Text 17
TEUN A. VAN DIJK: *Discourse as Structure and Process.*
Sage 1997, pages 22–3

This is a statement of principle from one of the leading proponents of critical discourse analysis. He explains that what makes discourse analysis critical is its commitment to a socio-political cause and makes it clear that those who follow this line are not merely academics but activists.

Finally, even when engaging in social discourse analysis, the analysts may do so in a distanced and disinterested way, trying to be 'objective', as the dominant norms of scholarship require. However, they may also become more actively involved in the topics and phenomena they study, as one would most probably do (whether intentionally or not) as soon as one studies power abuse, dominance and inequality as it is expressed or reproduced by discourse. The critical scholars make their social and political position explicit; they take sides, and actively participate in order to uncover, demystify or otherwise challenge dominance with their discourse analyses.

Instead of merely focusing on their discipline and its theories and paradigms, such discourse analysts focus on relevant social *problems*. That is, their work is more issue-oriented than theory-oriented. Analysis, description and theory formation play a role especially in as far as they allow better understanding and critique of social inequality, based on gender, ethnicity, class, origin, religion, language, sexual orientation and other criteria that define differences between people. Their ultimate goal is not only scientific, but also social and political, namely *change*. In that case, social discourse analysis takes the form of a *critical* discourse analysis.

▷ *Do you think that scholars have to 'take sides' to be 'actively involved in the topics and phenomena they study'?*

▷ *A distinction is made here between a focus on theory and a focus on 'relevant social problems', between 'issue-oriented' and 'theory-oriented' work. What is your view of the relationship between these?*

▷ *'Their ultimate goal is not only scientific, but also social and political, namely change.' Are these two goals always consistent with each other? Is social and political change always desirable?*

Text 18
ROGER FOWLER: *Linguistic Criticism*, 2nd edn.
Oxford University Press 1996, pages 34–5

This text and the one that follows are examples of critical discourse analysis. Fowler, a pioneer in this kind of work, developed it initially as an extension of literary criticism but

*applied to non-literary texts, and using, as he put it, a better
linguistic 'tool-kit'.*

The following three headlines appeared in the *Observer*, the
Sunday Times, and the *Sunday Telegraph* (respectively) on 12
December 1976:

1 NUS regrets fury over Joseph.
2 Student leaders condemn insult to Keith Joseph.
3 Student chiefs 'regret' attack on Sir Keith.

The headlines stand above reports of a sequence of events
involving the conference of the National Union of Students and
Sir Keith Joseph, at that time a member of the Conservative
opposition party in Parliament. On Friday, 10 December, Keith
Joseph had attempted to attend the conference as an observer,
was spotted, shouted at, and asked to leave after a voted decision
by the delegates that he should not be allowed to stay. All but two
members of the NUS executive had voted for his expulsion. The
next day, the executive issued a rather tongue-in-cheek statement
which might be taken to hint an apology to Keith Joseph. ...

On superficial examination, these three sentences all seem to
say the same thing. Yet they have noticeably different tonal
connotations—which are consistent with the political 'lines'
usually taken by the three newspapers—and on close scrutiny
appear ultimately to offer different analyses of the 'reality' they
report.

The different ways in which the participants are named are
significant: naming conventions are extremely regular and
revealing in English. The *Observer*'s 'Joseph' suggests formality
and distance; the *Sunday Telegraph*'s 'Sir' connotes respect while
the first name 'Keith' suggests intimacy. The connotations agree
with the papers' political characters: the *Observer* claims to be
liberal and is not likely to be in sympathy with Keith Joseph; the
Sunday Telegraph is a right-wing paper likely to admire such a
politician. The *Sunday Times*' 'Keith Joseph' seems to be neutral
and non-committal. The *Observer*'s 'NUS' makes it plain that the
paper recognizes the National Union of Students as a legitimate
organization well enough known to its readership to be identified
by initials. 'Student leaders' and 'student chiefs'—the latter phrase

with its implications of savagery or thuggery—are less sympathetic. The syntax of 'student leaders' could mean 'people who lead students' or 'people who are studying to be leaders' or 'students who lead students': the equivocation tends to undermine the status of the people referred to. Also 'student leaders', like 'student chiefs', evokes a range of comparable belittling phrases: 'petty tyrant', 'student nurse', 'junior officer', 'boy king', 'learner driver', etc.

These are fairly simple observations which require very little linguistics for their demonstration. But the fact is that we *do* respond to features such as these ...

▷ *'The connotations agree with the papers' political character.' How much do you think Fowler's interpretation of the different 'tonal connotations' of these headlines depends on knowing about the political stance of these papers beforehand?*

▷ *The ambiguous syntax of the phrase 'student leader' 'tends to undermine the status of the people referred to'. Can you explain why this should be so?*

▷ *The phrase 'student chiefs' is said to have 'implications of savagery and thuggery', and the two phrases 'student chiefs' and 'student leaders' to 'evoke comparable belittling phrases: 'petty tyrant', 'student nurse', etc. Do you agree?*

▷ *'The fact is that we do respond to features such as these.' Is it a fact that we respond to the features Fowler mentions? And do we all respond in the same way?*

Text 19

NORMAN FAIRCLOUGH: *Discourse and Social Change.* Polity Press 1992, pages 75–6

Fairclough's work has had an enormous influence on the development of critical discourse analysis (CDA). Like Fowler, he takes the view that specific linguistic features of a text can be interpreted as representing a particular attitude. Here, in a typical example of his procedure, he considers the significance of certain grammatical aspects of a newspaper headline.

The main unit of grammar is the clause, or 'simple sentence', for example the newspaper headline 'Gorbachev Rolls Back the Red Army'. The main elements of clauses are usually called 'groups' or 'phrases', for example 'the Red Army', 'Rolls Back'. Clauses combine to make up complex sentences. My comments here will be restricted to certain aspects of the clause.

Every clause is multifunctional, and so every clause is a combination of ideational, interpersonal (identity and relational), and textual meanings ... People make choices about the design and structure of their clauses which amount to choices about how to signify (and construct) social identities, social relationships, and knowledge and belief. Let me illustrate with the newspaper headline above. In terms of ideational meaning, the clause is transitive: it signifies a process of a particular individual acting physically (note the metaphor) upon an entity. We might well see here a different ideological investment from other ways of signifying the same events, for example 'The Soviet Union Reduces its Armed Forces', or 'The Soviet Army Gives up 5 Divisions'. In terms of interpersonal meaning, the clause is declarative (as opposed to interrogative, or imperative), and contains a present tense form of the verb which is categorically authoritative. The writer-reader relationship here is that between someone telling what is the case in no uncertain terms, and someone being told; these are the two subject positions set up in the clause. Thirdly, there is the textual aspect: 'Gorbachev' is topic or theme of the clause, as the first part of a clause usually is: the article is about him and his doings. On the other hand, if the clause were made into a passive, that would make 'the Red Army' the theme: 'The Red Army is Rolled Back (by Gorbachev)'. Another possibility offered by the passive is the deletion of the (bracketed) agent, because the agent is unknown, already known, judged irrelevant, or perhaps in order to leave agency and hence responsibility vague.

▷ *The central problem in discourse analysis, according to Labov (Text 1) and others (e.g. Gee in Text 9), is inferring what is done from what is said. Fairclough here, and Fowler in Text 18, do not seem to find this problematic. Are they doing a different kind of discourse analysis?*

▷ *'We might well see here a different ideological investment from other ways of signifying the same events.' What different ideological investment do you see in the alternative wordings that Fairclough provides?*

▷ *'... the present tense form of the verb ... is categorically authoritative.' What do you think is meant by that?*

▷ *Can you suggest what difference there would be in 'ideological investment' if the headline was rewritten in the passive with or without deleting the agent (by Gorbachev)?*

Text 20

KIERAN O'HALLORAN: *Critical Discourse Analysis and Language Cognition*. Edinburgh University Press 2003, page 3

Fowler says (Text 18) that we as readers 'do respond' to the kind of features that he identifies as significant. But do we? O'Halloran raises the question here of how far the meanings that the analyst spends time and effort extracting out of a text correspond with how readers actually interpret it. In the preceding text, for example, Fairclough points to the possible significance of the absence of an agent in a passive sentence, but what if the reader would not normally notice such an absence?

It is safe to assume that critical discourse analysts spend quite some time in the analysis of text and that this must involve a much higher degree of effort than that invested by, say, readers who are reading for gist. This is particularly the case if analysts are pointing out absences from a sentence which, for them, mean the event being reported is mystified for the gist reader; analysing absences from a sentence in a text is not part of reading for gist. But all this begs the following question, one which is seldom addressed in CDA: how can analysts be sure that the absences from a sentence they detect would not be generated as inferences anyway via other information in the text? This leads on to more general questions. For example, to what extent is the interpretation a critical discourse analyst makes from a text on behalf of a non-analyst dependent on the longer amount of time and thus larger amount of effort the analyst invests? How do analysts know that they are not *over-interpreting* on behalf of readers, who, in reading only for gist, would not invest the same amount of effort? It is not surprising that such questions do not usually occupy critical discourse analysts. Because developments in CDA over the last fifteen years or so have been largely related to linking linguistic analysis with sociocultural analysis, anything to do with cognition in the interpretation stage has not received comprehensive scrutiny. Assumptions in CDA for how readers operate are largely intuitive or undeveloped. Indeed, CDA is largely unaware that it possesses a number of tensions with regard to how it treats the cognition of texts.

▷ *O'Halloran says that the way a text is analysed does not correspond with the way people process it when reading for gist. Does this invalidate the analysis?*

▷ *'How do analysts know that they are not over-interpreting on behalf of readers, who, in reading only for gist would not invest the same amount of effort?' How do you think the CDA analyst might reply to this question?*

▷ *Why should it be the case, as O'Halloran suggests, that CDA's 'linking linguistic analysis with sociocultural analysis' leads to a neglect of 'cognition at the interpretation stage'?*

Chapter 8
Text analysis

Text 21
SUSAN HUNSTON: *Corpora in Applied Linguistics*. Cambridge: Cambridge University Press 2002, pages 143,145–6

Corpus analysis reveals regularities in the patterns of language in texts over and above those which are determined by grammar. This text refers to such patterns as 'phraseologies' and discusses them in relation to the 'idiom principle' as proposed by Sinclair in his book Corpus, Concordance, Collocation *(Oxford University Press, 1991).*

If we look at English from the point of view of the words that make it up, then, each word can be described in terms of its preferred phraseologies. Mostly, though, users of a language encounter that language as a piece of speaking or writing, not as a set of concordance lines. Sinclair (1991) argues that much of what appears in spoken or written texts follows what he calls the 'idiom principle', that is each word in the text is used in a common phraseology, meaning is attached to the whole phrase rather than to the individual parts of it, and the hearer or reader understands the phrase as a phrase rather than as a grammatical template with lexical items in it. When a stretch of language cannot be interpreted in the light of the idiom principle, the language user falls back on the 'open-choice principle', following which principle words are much less predictable …

Sinclair suggests that any group or sequence of words is constructed and understood in the light of one or other of these principles, but not both. In other words, meaning is made either by the phrase as a whole, operating in accordance with the conventional phraseology, or (less often) it is made by individual words, operating in accordance with grammatical rules. The choice between the idiom or open-choice principles makes ambiguity theoretically possible; the fact that either one or the other is employed by the language user at any one time explains why ambiguity is rarely a problem for speakers and hearers. For example, *grasp the point* is in theory ambiguous. Interpreted according to the idiom principle, it means ' understand the main idea of something'; interpreted according to the open-choice principle, with *GRASP* combining with anything indicating a solid object, it means 'take hold of the sharp end of something'. In practice, however, only one interpretation is activated, and few readers will be undecided as to which meaning is intended in a sentence such as: *Perhaps, finally, this terrible accident will help the islanders grasp the point.*

▷ *Do you think the term 'phraseology' as used in this text means the same as 'collocation' as discussed in Chapter 8, or something different?*

▷ *Do you agree that ambiguity can be explained by reference to the choice between the idiom and open-choice principles as described in this text?*

▷ *'In practice, however, only one interpretation is activated'. What activates the use of one principle rather than the other? What part, if any, do you think context has to play?*

▷ *Refer to Hymes' model of communicative competence in Text 5. How far would it be true to say that the open-choice principle relates to what is possible, and the idiom principle to what is actually performed?*

Text 22

DOUGLAS BIBER, SUSAN CONRAD, and RANDI REPPEN: *Corpus Linguistics. Investigating Language Structure and Use.* Cambridge University Press 1998, pages 107–8

Although it is conceded that not all aspects of discourse can be automatically analysed by computer, there are certain aspects that can be, and corpus analysis in this case can provide a means for the identification and comparison of the typical linguistic properties of particular varieties of text, here referred to as 'register'.

There are several reasons why discourse studies have generally not been corpus-based in the past. First, many discourse features cannot be identified automatically. The analysis of such features is often labor-intensive, requiring detailed consideration of language features in their larger textual contexts. For example, one goal of discourse analysis is to classify the kinds of information in a text, usually focusing on noun phrases as the primary carriers of referential information. Such analyses attempt to determine which pieces of information are already 'known' by the reader/ listener, versus those noun phrases that present 'new ' information. It is impossible to make distinctions of this type automatically; the discourse analyst must consider the previous textual context, and in some cases analysts even consider the background knowledge that readers/listeners use to understand a text. As a result, it requires a large commitment of time and energy to analyze extended texts in this way ...

Difficulties such as these might be taken to suggest that the corpus-based approach is not useful for discourse studies, and it is simply not feasible to attempt broader studies with generalizable results. However, there are two major ways in which a corpus-based approach can be used to investigate discourse features. First, it is possible to develop and use interactive computer programs (similar to a spellchecker) to analyze discourse characteristics. Such programs can identify certain discourse characteristics more reliably and faster than humans can, while at the same time providing a means for the researcher to make judgements about areas that cannot be analyzed automatically. Second, it is possible to use automatic analyses to track the use of grammatical features over the course of a text. These analyses actually map the development of discourse patterns through texts; they can be used to compare texts, to find the typical patterns for a register, or to see how a particular text compares to the general pattern for the register.

▷ *'many discourse features cannot be identified automatically'. The authors give one example. Can you suggest others? What kind of discourse feature is being referred to here?*

▷ *Computer programs 'can identify certain discourse characteristics more reliably and faster than humans can'. What kind of discourse characteristics would these be? Is a distinction being made here, do you think, between 'discourse features' and 'discourse characteristics'?*

▷ *'These analyses actually map the development of discourse patterns through texts.' What kind of patterns would these be?*

▷ *The terms 'discourse' and 'text' occur frequently in this passage. Do they mean the same thing, or are they meant to refer to different concepts?*

SECTION 3
References

The references which follow can be classified into introductory level (marked ■□□), more advanced and consequently more technical (marked ■■□), and specialized, very demanding (marked ■■■)

General introductions
Linguistic perspective: focus on discourse as language use

■■□

ROBERT de BEAUGRANDE and WOLFGANG DRESSLER: *Introduction to Text Linguistics*. Longman 1981

■■□

GILLIAN BROWN and GEORGE YULE: *Discourse Analysis*. Cambridge University Press 1983

■□□

DEBORAH CAMERON: *Working with Spoken Discourse*. Sage 2001

■□□

MALCOLM COULTHARD: *An Introduction to Discourse Analysis* (2nd edn). Longman 1984

■■□

DEBORAH SCHIFFRIN: *Approaches to Discourse*. Blackwell 1994

Socio-cultural perspective: focus on discourse as social practice

■■□

JAN BLOMMAERT: *Discourse: A Critical Introduction.* Cambridge University Press 2005

■□□

JAMES PAUL GEE: *An Introduction to Discourse Analysis: Theory and Method.* Routledge 1999 (see Text 9)

■□□

SARA MILLS: *Discourse.* Routledge 2004

Multiple perspectives:

■■■

DEBORAH SCHIFFRIN, DEBORAH TANNEN, and HEIDI H. HAMILTON (eds.): *The Handbook of Discourse Analysis.* Blackwell 2001

Chapter 1
Language in use

■■□

GUY COOK: *The Discourse of Advertising* (2nd edn). Routledge 2001 (see Text 3)

Chapter 4 ('Language and paralanguage') explains the significance of paralinguistic features in both spoken and written language use.

■■□

DEBORAH SCHIFFRIN: *Approaches to Discourse.* Blackwell 1994

Chapter 2 ('Definitions of discourse') identifies two essentially different ways of defining the nature of discourse: the formalist or structuralist way which defines it as language above the sentence, and the functionalist way which defines it as language in use.

■■□

H. G. WIDDOWSON: *Text, Context, Pretext*. Blackwell 2004

The first chapter elaborates on the distinction between text and discourse.

■□□

GEORGE YULE: *Pragmatics*. Oxford University Press 1996.

An accessible but detailed introduction which focuses particularly on the pragmatics of spoken interaction.

Chapter 2
Communication

■□□

J. L. AUSTIN: *How to Do Things with Words*.
Oxford University Press 1975

This very readable exploration of how language is used in communication inspired later work on speech act theory and the pragmatics of discourse generally from a philosophical point of view.

■■□

D.H. HYMES: 'On communicative competence'
in J. B. Pride and Janet Holmes (eds.) *Sociolinguistics*.
Penguin Books 1972 (see Text 5)

A seminal and much-cited paper that points to what is involved in being communicatively competent in a language beyond a knowledge of the encoded properties of the language itself. A key work in understanding the nature of discourse.

■■□

WILLIAM LABOV: 'The study of language in its social context' in *Sociolinguistic Patterns*. Basil Blackwell 1972 (see Text 11)

Like Hymes, Labov shifted the focus of attention from language as a formal encoded system in the abstract to how it actually occurs in contexts of use.

■■□

JOHN SEARLE: *Speech Acts*. Cambridge University Press 1969 (see Text 6)

Another classic work, which develops the insights of Austin into a theory of speech acts. Enquiries into the nature of linguistic communication were taking place on two fronts at the same time: in the philosophical work of Austin and Searle on the one hand, and in the sociolinguistic work of Hymes and Labov on the other.

Chapter 3
Context

■■■

P. AUER and A. DI LUZIO (eds.) *The Contextualization of Language*. John Benjamins 1992

This is a collection of papers that deals not with context as a state of affairs or a state of mind, but with contextualization as a process of online adaptation, and so part of the negotiation of meaning.

■■■

J. R. FIRTH: 'Personality and language in society' in *Papers in Linguistics (1934–51)*. Oxford University Press 1957

This paper presents Firth's attempt to develop Malinowski's original notion of context of situation (see Text 8) into a contextual theory of meaning.

■■■

DAN SPERBER and DIERDRE WILSON: *Relevance: Communication and Cognition* (2nd edn). Blackwell 1995 (see Text 10)

Context is dealt with here as a cognitive construct and is central to the development in this book of a theory of discourse meaning based on the concept of relevance.

■■□

H. G. WIDDOWSON: *Text, Context, Pretext*. Blackwell 2004

Chapters 3 and 4 are devoted to a consideration of the notion of context, as defined by various authors, and its relationship with co-text.

Chapter 4
Schematic conventions

■■□

F.G. BARTLETT: *Remembering*.
Cambridge University Press 1932

An influential book in its time which put forward innovative ideas about the nature of the schema and its effect on memory. Still often cited as seminal.

■□□

GUY COOK: *Discourse and Literature*.
Oxford University Press 1994

The first chapter here gives a particularly clear account of schema theory and its role in the interpretation of discourse.

■■□

STEPHEN LEVINSON: *Pragmatics*.
Cambridge University Press 1983

Chapter 6 gives a detailed account of turn taking and the routine conventions for the structuring of conversational interaction.

■■■

A. J. SANFORD and S. C. GARROD: *Understanding Written Language*. John Wiley & Sons 1981 (see Text 12)

A detailed and comprehensive enquiry into ways in which schematic knowledge affects the interpretation of written text.

■■□

JOHN SWALES: *Genre Analysis*. Cambridge University Press 1990

Although particularly concerned with English, and with English as it is used in academic settings, Part II of this book explores the concepts of discourse community and genre in more general terms.

Chapter 5
Co-textual relations

■■□

GILLIAN BROWN and GEORGE YULE: *Discourse Analysis.* Cambridge University Press 1983

Chapter 6 gives a clear and comprehensive account of text cohesion, as distinct from discourse coherence, which is dealt with in Chapter 7 of the book.

■■■

WOLFRAM BUBLITZ, UTA LENK, and EIJA VENTOLA (eds.): *Coherence in Spoken and Written Discourse.* John Benjamins 1999

A collection of essays which includes a detailed bibliography of coherence and cohesion.

■■■

M. A. K HALLIDAY: *An Introduction to Functional Grammar* (2nd edn). Edward Arnold 1994

This full and authoritative statement of Halliday's theory of grammar provides a detailed account of information structure in Chapter 8, and of cohesion in Chapter 9.

■■□

M. A. K HALLIDAY and RUQUAIYA HASAN: *Cohesion in English.* Longman 1976 (see Text 14)

This still remains the most detailed description of the different linguistic devices available in English for making connection within texts to make them cohesive.

■■■

J. R. MARTIN: 'Cohesion and texture' in Deborah Schiffrin, Deborah Tannen, and Heidi H. Hamilton (eds.) *The Handbook of Discourse Analysis.* Blackwell 2001

A development of the ideas of Halliday and Hasan on cohesion in text. The article also includes an extensive bibliography.

■■□

MICHAEL STUBBS: *Words and Phrases*. Blackwell 2001

This book uses the procedures of corpus analysis to demonstrate how the meaning of words can be derived from regularities of their co-textual occurrence. A number of case studies are provided which demonstrate the relationship between collocation, cohesion, and coherence.

Chapter 6
The negotiation of meaning

■■□

H. P. GRICE: 'Logic and conversation' in P. Cole and J. Morgan (eds.) *Syntax and Semantics* vol. 3, *Speech Acts*. Academic Press 1975 (see Text 15)

The original formulation of the co-operative principle and its four conversational maxims.

■□□

JENNY THOMAS: *Meaning in Interaction: An Introduction to Pragmatics*. 1995. Longman

Chapter 3 is a particularly clear and readable discussion of implicature, the co-operative principle, and the conversational maxims, and Chapter 4 then discusses problems that arise from Grice's proposals and relates them to Searle's speech act theory.

Chapter 7
Critical approaches

■□□

NORMAN FAIRCLOUGH: *Language and Power* (2nd edn). Longman 2001

Perhaps the clearest and most accessible account of the principles and practices of critical discourse analysis by the scholar who is probably its most influential proponent.

■■■

NORMAN FAIRCLOUGH: *Discourse and Social Change.*
Polity Press 1992 (see Text 19)

This is a complex book. It begins with an account of different approaches to discourse analysis and then goes on to propose a social theory of discourse, followed by a demonstration of how the theory applies to actual analysis.

■■■

KIERAN O'HALLORAN: *Critical Discourse Analysis and Language Cognition.* Edinburgh University Press 2003 (see Text 20)

This book points to problems with CDA procedures for assigning significance in their analysis of texts and argues that more account needs to be taken of the cognitive factors that come into play in interpretation.

■□□

BARBARA SEIDLHOFER: *Controversies in Applied Linguistics.* Oxford University Press 2003

Section 3 deals with controversies concerning critical discourse analysis. A particularly clear and well-referenced account of the main issues involved prepares the ground for the presentation of previously published texts expressing opposing positions.

■■■

STEFAN TITSCHER, MICHAEL MEYER, RUTH WODAK, and EVA VETTER: *Methods of Text and Discourse Analysis.* Sage Publications 2000

A detailed and demanding survey of different methods of text analysis. It distinguishes between Fairclough's text-oriented approach to critical discourse analysis and the 'discourse-historical method' developed by Wodak and her colleagues, which places particular emphasis on context.

Chapter 8
Text analysis

■■□

GRAEME KENNEDY: *An Introduction to Corpus Linguistics.*
Longman 1998.

A comprehensive overview of how language corpora have been
designed and developed with an account of the procedures of
corpus analysis as applied to descriptions of English.

■□□

MIKE SCOTT and CHRISTOPHER TRIBBLE:
Textual Patterns. John Benjamins 2005

The first part of this book provides a very clear introduction to
the scope of corpus analysis, dealing with such basic issues as
word frequency, collocation, and the concept of the key word.
The second part illustrates what corpus analysis can reveal when
applied to different kinds of text.

■■□

MICHAEL STUBBS: *Text and Corpus Analysis.*
Blackwell 1996

The first part of this book deals with general concepts of text
analysis with a focus on their historical development. The second
part presents examples of how corpus analysis can be applied to
particular texts, and enquires into what implications the findings
might have for their interpretation.

■■■

ALISON WRAY: *Formulaic Language and the Lexicon.*
Cambridge University Press 2002

A very comprehensive enquiry into the nature of formulaic
sequences in language use in general, with detailed discussion of
their occurrence in first and second language acquisition.

Apart from the particular works cited above, reference can also be made to the relevant entries in encyclopedias of language and linguistics in general.

■■■

KEITH BROWN (editor-in-chief): *Encyclopedia of Language and Linguistics* (2nd edn) (14 volumes). Elsevier 1996

■■□

WILLIAM J. FRAWLEY (editor-in-chief): *International Encyclopedia of Linguistics* (2nd edn) (4 volumes). Oxford University Press 2003

■□□

DAVID CRYSTAL: *The Cambridge Encyclopedia of Language* (2nd edn) (1 volume). Cambridge University Press 1997

SECTION 4
Glossary

Page numbers of references in SECTION 1 (Survey) are given at the end of each entry.

adjacency pair A pair of utterances in conversation of which the second is a conventional response to the first, e.g. *question/answer*. [37]

ambiguity The convergence of two grammatical structures into one to create a double meaning. [14]

anaphora The use of a term as a **pro-form** to make a textual connection to something previously referred to, e.g. *The Prime Minister arrived. He ...* where the pronoun *he* makes **anaphoric** reference to *The Prime Minister*. [44]

appropriate Related to context in a conventionally accepted way. Knowing whether and to what extent an expression is appropriate to context is one of the four aspects of **communicative competence** as defined by Hymes. [12]

cataphoric Whereas in **anaphoric** reference the **pro-form** refers to what comes earlier in a text, with cataphoric reference it refers to what comes later, e.g. *When he arrived, the Prime Minister ...* [47]

coherence (adj. **coherent**) The interpretation of a **text** so that it makes sense. A feature of **discourse 1**. [49]

cohesion The linking together of parts of a **text** by means of **pro-forms** of various kinds. [45] **Cohesive devices** link together parts of a text. [46]

collocation The co-occurrence of words in **text**, e.g. the word *unforeseen* regularly **collocates** with the word *circumstances*; the word *dense* collocates with *fog* but not with *soup*. [16, 79]

comment The **rheme** interpreted as what **P1** wants to say on a topic. [43]

communicative competence As defined by Hymes (see Text 5), the knowledge of what constitutes the communicative use of language and which enables users to make judgements about how far a particular use is **possible, feasible, appropriate,** and **performed.** [14]

concordance The display of the different **co-texts** of occurrence of particular words, typically the result of the computer analysis of a **corpus.** [80]

connotation Suggestive meaning: the associations that are called up by a word, e.g. *lion* suggests bravery in many people's minds. [69]

constituent A component part of the **sentence** as identified by grammatical analysis e.g. the sentence *Old men forget* is said to consist of a noun phrase constituent *old men* and a verb phrase constituent *forget*. [3]

context Aspects of extra-linguistic reality that are taken to be relevant to communication. [4]

conversational implicature Meaning that is not explicitly expressed but implied by the violation of the **co-operative principle,** e.g. if I were to say *My brother is a pig* you would recognize this as untrue, and suppose that I was therefore implying something else. [58]

co-operative imperative The instinctive need for people to make contact and co-operate with others. [64]

co-operative principle As proposed by Grice, a shared assumption by the parties in a conversation that they will co-operate with each other for the purpose of their talk by keeping to certain conventional **maxims.** [56]

corpus A collection, often on a very large scale, of actually occurring textual data, electronically stored and analysable by computer program. [78]

co-text The internal linkage of linguistic elements within a text. See **cohesion.** [44]

co-textual relations The internal relations that linguistic elements contract with each other within a text. [41]

critical discourse analysis (CDA) A socio-politically motivated approach to the study of language in use that generally assigns ideological significance to texts on the basis of their linguistic features. [70]

declarative knowledge Knowledge that can be made explicit and talked about. Cf. **procedural knowledge.** [17]

deixis The use of a term to make an external reference to the immediate **situation.** Cf. **Anaphora.** [27]

denotation (verb **denote**) The **semantic meaning** of words encoded in a language. Cf. **reference.** [4]

discourse 1), as discussed generally in this book, the meaning that a first person intends to express in producing a text, and that a second person interprets from the text. 2), as a **CDA** concept, a mode of social practice: a set of socio-cultural conventions for conceiving of reality in certain ways and controlling it. [6]

discourse community A group of people who subscribe to the conventions that define a particular kind of language use or **genre.** [40]

encoding conventions Conventions that have established what aspects of reality are encoded by what linguistic forms in a particular language. See **semantics.** [11]

face Personal self-image made public. [64]

feasibility One of Hymes' aspects of communication: the degree to which a linguistic form can be decoded or processed. See **communicative competence.** [14]

formally encoded Encoded as a linguistic form. [11]

formulaic phrase A frequently recurring **collocation** of relatively fixed sequence and form. Some such phrases are completely fixed, e.g. *By and large, Be that as it may,* while others allow for varying degrees of flexibility. [80]

frame of reference A familiar representation of reality. See **ideational schema.** [29]

genre A use of language which conforms to certain schematic and textual conventions, as agreed by a particular **discourse community.** [38]

given The **theme** interpreted as giving information already known to **P2.** Cf. **new.** [42]

grammatical well-formedness Conformity to the established and accepted rules of grammar. What is grammatically well-formed corresponds, in Hymes' terms, to what is **possible** in a language. [12]

ideational schema (*pl.* **schemata**) A mental construct of reality or **frame of reference** which represents a customary and predictable way of seeing things. See **schema**. [33]

illocutionary act What is done when something is said. The use of language to perform a recognized act of communication, e.g. a promise, a warning. What is said then takes on a certain communicative value or **illocutionary force**. [13]

interpersonal routines Procedures for managing spoken interaction that are established as customary in a particular community. See **interpersonal schemata**. [33]

interpersonal schemata Accepted conventions for structuring communication generally and comprising both the routines of spoken interaction and the **genres** of written language use. [33]

lexical item A separate unit of meaning, usually, but not necessarily, corresponding with a word. [13]

lexis The words and phrases of a language as units of **semantic** meaning. [9]

linguistic competence The knowledge of a language as a formal system, of what is linguistically encoded—a knowledge, in Hymes' terms, of the **possible**. [11]

maxims These are the four tenets of the **co-operative principle**. The quantity maxim relates to amount of information provided, the quality maxim to its truth, the relation maxim to its relevance, and the manner maxim to how it is expressed. (See Text 15.) [56]

multimodality (adj. **multimodal**) The combination and complex interplay of verbal text with visual and aural means of signifying in different kinds of communication, e.g. the pictures and print in advertisements, the soundtrack and visual effects in film. [8]

new The **rheme** interpreted as giving new information to **P2**. Cf. **given**. [43]

P1 The first-person party or addresser (*I, we*), the text producer. [22, 42]

P2 The second-person party or addressee (*you*), the text receiver. [22, 42]

paralanguage Non-linguistic ways of signalling meaning that accompany and act upon the verbal text, e.g. gesture, facial expression, 'tone of voice' in speech, the size and placement of print in written language use. [8]

performed Actually produced language behaviour. Knowing the extent to which an expression is performed is, according to Hymes, part of **communicative competence**. [16]

perlocutionary effect The effect that a particular **illocutionary act** has on the second-person receiver, e.g. the effect of a promise might be to reassure somebody, or persuade them to act in a certain way. [13]

position The attitude or point of view taken up by P1 in producing a text, or by P2 in interpreting it. [24, 65, 67]

possible Conforming to the encoding conventions of a language. Thus, every sentence generated by established grammatical rule is possible. Knowing what is possible is what constitutes **linguistic competence** and is one aspect of Hymes' account of **communicative competence**. [14]

pragmatic meaning What language users make of language use, i.e. what a **P1** means by a text and what a text means to a **P2**. See **reference**. Cf. **semantic meaning**. [8]

procedural knowledge Know-how: a knowledge of how to do something without being able to explain it. Cf. **declarative knowledge**. [17]

pro-form A linguistic form that stands in for another expression in a text by copying some of its **semantic features**. Thus in *The taxi has been ordered. It will be here in a minute*, the pronoun *it* copies the features of singular/inanimate from the noun *taxi*. See **anaphora**. [44]

proposition What is referred to in an utterance. [12]

quantity maxim See **maxims**.

range The extent to which the occurrence of a word is distributed across different domains of use and kinds of text. [78]

reference (verb **refer**) The use of language to talk about things in context. A pragmatic function. People refer by means of words, but the words themselves do not refer. Cf. **denotation**. [4]

rheme (R) The second part of a proposition, taking the form of the rest of the sentence after the first constituent, e.g. *Ants/ infested the house(R). The house/was infested with ants(R).* [41]

schema (*pl.* **schemata**) A mental construct of taken-for-granted assumptions about how reality is ordered (**ideational schemata**) and how communication is managed (**interpersonal schemata**). [26]

schematic knowledge Knowledge of the schemata that are operative within a particular community of language users. Cf. **systemic knowledge**. [53]

semantic feature Element of meaning encoded within a **lexical item**, e.g. *woman* encodes the features female/human/singular. [9, 44]

semantic meaning Meaning that is linguistically encoded in the **lexis** and grammar of a language. See **denotation**. Cf. **pragmatic meaning**. [8]

semantic prosody Meaning that extends from one word in a **collocation** to another, e.g. the word *cause* usually **collocates** with words denoting unpleasant things like *difficulty*, *distress*, *trouble*, and so on, and is therefore said to have a **negative semantic prosody**. Conversely, *bring about*, which collocates frequently with words like *improvement*, *solution*, *success*, and so on, is said to have a **positive semantic prosody**. [81]

sentence A unit of grammatical analysis usually consisting of a noun phrase and a verb phrase. *See* **constituent**. [3]

service encounter An everyday transaction in which some kind of service is provided, e.g. face to face at a restaurant or hotel reception desk, or by telephone at a call centre. [33]

situation The actual circumstances of time and place in which a use of language is located. [19]

speech event Familiar and routine kinds of language use, e.g. an interview, a lecture, a **service encounter**. [38]

systemic knowledge Knowledge of a language as an encoded system, of what in Hymes' terms is **possible** in a language. Cf. **schematic knowledge**. [53]

terms of address Terms used by **P1** to address **P2**, e.g. *Mr President, Your honour*, the pronoun *you*. [34]

terms of reference Terms used by **P1** to refer to a third person, e.g. *The President, His honour*, the pronouns *he/she/they*. [68]

territorial imperative The instinctive need of people to secure and protect their own space. Cf. **co-operative imperative**. [64]

text The language produced by P1 in the communication process. The linguistic trace in speech or writing of P1's intended **discourse**. [4]

textualize To give explicit linguistic expression in text to intended meaning rather than leaving it implicit and to be inferred from context. [7]

theme (T) The first part of a **proposition**. It takes the form of the first constituent of the **sentence**, e.g. *Ants(T)/infested the house, The house (T)/was infested with ants*. [41]

topic The **theme** interpreted as what **P1** wants to talk about. Cf. **comment**. [43]

utterance A communicative use of language which takes on pragmatic meaning. The term usually refers to short expressions in spoken language like turns in a conversation. Cf. **sentence**. [8, 13]

Acknowledgements

The authors and publisher are grateful to those who have given permission to reproduce the following extracts and adaptations of copyright material:

Blackwell Publishing for permission to reproduce extracts from *Text and Corpus Analysis* by Michael Stubbs published in 1996 by Blackwell Publishing.

Cambridge University Press for permission to reproduce extracts from: *Discourse Analysis* by Gillian Brown and George Yule (1983); *Speech Acts* by John Searle (1969); *Pragmatics* by Stephen C. Levinson (1983); extracts from *Corpus Linguistics* by Douglas Biber, Susan Conrad, and Randi Reppen (1998); *Corpora in Applied Linguistics* by Susan E. Hunston (2002), reprinted by permission of Cambridge University Press and the author.

Edinburgh University Press for permission to reproduce extracts from *Critical Discourse Analysis and Language Cognition* by Kieran O'Halloran, 2003.

Elsevier for permission to reproduce extracts from 'Logic and Conversation' by H.P. Grice from *Syntax and Semantics Volume 3: Speech Acts* © 1975.

The *Independent* for permission to reproduce extracts from 'Muslim Council Checks for Extremists' from *The Independent* 15 August 2005 © The *Independent* 2005.

The National Council of Teachers of English for permission to reprint extracts from *The Study of Non-Standard English* by William Labov © 1969 The National Council of Teachers of English.

The *New Statesman* for permission to reproduce extracts from 'Learn among the chickens' by Rachel Aspden from the *New Statesman* 27 September 2004; 'Europe's very own Puerto Rico' by Tom Gallagher from the *New Statesman* 6 September 2004.

Oxford University Press for permission to reproduce extracts from *Linguistic Criticism 2nd edition* by Roger Fowler. Oxford

University Press, Inc. for permission to reproduce extracts from 2003 *International Encyclopaedia of Linguistics* 2nd edition.

Pearson Education Limited for permission to reproduce extracts from *Cohesion in English* by M.A.K. Halliday and R. Hasan © 1976 Pearson Education Limited.

Polity Press for permission to reproduce extracts from *Discourse and Social Change* by Norman Fairclough.

Routledge for permission to reproduce: extracts from page 71 of *The Discourse of Advertising* by G Cook (2001); pages 62–3 of *An Introduction to Discourse Analysis, Theory and Method* by James Paul Gee (1999); pages 120–22 of *Textual Interaction: An Introduction to Discourse Analysis* by Michael Hoey (2001).

Sage Publications for permission to reproduce extracts from *Discourse as Structure and Process* by Teun A Van Dijk.

The Society of Authors, on behalf of the Bernard Shaw Estate, for permission to reproduce extracts from *Pygmalion* by George Bernard Shaw.

Dan Sperber and Deirdre Wilson for permission to reproduce extracts from *Relevance: Communication and Cognition* 2nd edition. Reprinted by kind permission of the authors.

The University of Pennsylvania Press for permission to reproduce extracts from 'On Communicative Competence' by D. H Hymes from *Sociolinguistcs* © 1972 University of Pennsylvania Press; and for permission to reproduce extracts from *Sociolinguistc Patterns* by William Labov © 1972 University of Pennsylvania Press.

John Wiley and Sons Ltd. for permission to reproduce extracts from *Understanding Written Language* by A.J. Sanford and S.C. Garrod © 1981.

Although every effort has been made to trace and contact copyright holders before publication, this has not been possible in some cases. We apologize for any apparent infringement of copyright and if notified, the publisher will be pleased to rectify any errors or omissions at the earliest opportunity.